Multigenerational Communication in Organizations

Multigenerational Communication in Organizations explores generational differences in the changing workplace from a communication perspective.

Starting from the reality that a workplace can contain up to five different generations, these chapters examine topics like generational perceptions on the job search process; organizational culture; organizational identification; organizational crises; the dark side of workplace communication; remote working; and future challenges. Outlines of best practices and suggestions for application are provided based on the most recent data and corresponding literature. The authors also develop a data-forward understanding of Generation Z in context.

This book is ideal for both scholars and practitioners in organizational communication and management, as well as for workplace managers and supervisors.

Michael G. Strawser is an Assistant Professor of Communication at the University of Central Florida.

Stephanie A. Smith is an Assistant Professor of Communication at Virginia Tech.

Bridget Rubenking is an Associate Professor of Communication at the University of Central Florida.

Routledge Focus on Communication Studies

Multigenerational Communication in Organizations
Insights from the Workplace

Michael G. Strawser,
Stephanie A. Smith, and
Bridget Rubenking

Routledge
Taylor & Francis Group

NEW YORK AND LONDON

First published 2021
by Routledge
605 Third Avenue, New York, NY 10158

and by Routledge
2 Park Square, Milton Park, Abingdon, Oxon, OX14 4RN

Routledge is an imprint of the Taylor & Francis Group, an
informa business

Library of Congress Cataloging-in-Publication Data
A catalog record for this title has been requested

ISBN: 978-0-367-71428-4 (hbk)
ISBN: 978-0-367-71430-7 (pbk)
ISBN: 978-1-003-15083-1 (ebk)

Typeset in Times New Roman
by MPS Limited, Dehradun

Contents

Tables

viii *Tables*

1 The Evolving Organization

Generally, organizations and corporations consistently evolve and change. For the purposes of this volume, we approach organizational change through a generational lens. Meaning, throughout this book we examine the changing organization by focusing on people within the organization. Organizations are dynamic organisms that, at times, include four or five generations working together under one umbrella. This dynamic can be encouraging, enlightening, and engaging. Yet, if not approached correctly and effectively, generational differences in organizations can cause dissent and disruption. Through our own research and prior literature, we demonstrate that a data-driven understanding of generational differences of Baby Boomers, Generation X, Millennials, and members of Generation Z, relating to workplace-specific variables, can help us understand the 21st century organization in a new and unique way. This book addresses the following organizational variables: the job search, organizational culture, organizational identification, mentorship and supportive workplace communication, dissent and conflict, workplace satisfaction, and remote or virtual work through a generational perspective. We believe a data-driven understanding of generational differences, relating to these workplace-specific variables, can help us understand the 21st century organization in a new and unique way.

The remainder of Chapter 1 investigates the changing organization and previews our study. In Chapter 2, we explore the differences and similarities among the generations in the workplace. Chapter 3 positions communication as an integral feature of the organization. This chapter also sets the foundation for the remainder of the book. In Chapter 4, we begin to address topics specific to our study and previous research. Specifically, Chapter 4 discusses generational differences in the job search process. Chapter 5 describes differing perspectives on organizational culture. In Chapter 6, we offer findings on organizational identification and belonging. Chapter 7 and Chapter 8 describe different perspectives on communication in the organization, first exploring positive communication and then detailing different perceptions of the dark side of communication in organizations. Chapter 9 explores workplace satisfaction. Chapters 10 and Chapter 11 discuss more future-oriented ideas like remote work and innovation. Chapter 11 also attempts to describe the future of work. While the chapters are, primarily, research-related we have used this space to also identify some best practices that may be helpful for those leading and managing generational teams. As we dive into generational differences in the workplace, it is important to first understand how the organization has changed and why the modern, or 21st century organization, functions as it does.

1.1 Investigating Organizational Change

It is difficult to conceptualize how organizations evolve. For one, organizations are living, breathing organisms (Arghode, Jandu, & McLean, 2020). They are not stagnant. Organizations grow, develop, die, and change. For some, organizations have been defined according to academic foci and theories of management. The dominant concept of the 1960s, McGregor's Theory X and Theory Y, situated two different work styles and approaches to work itself. McGregor (1960) believes people will be motivated by either a carrot or a stick and that most individuals have an inherent dislike for work or will value work itself. The emphasis was on the worker, the employee, the individual. The manager, during this time, had to come to a more robust understanding of the human factor, or those relational elements that manifest themselves in the workplace. The 1970s was a strategic renaissance, as the SWOT analysis and strategic planning rose to prominence (Stait, 1972). The emphasis was still on the human factor, but managers assumed even inept employees could be overcome by a proper system and strategy. In the 1980s, organizations started to take their strategy and develop true systems, in many ways lean systems, that accomplished more with less and tried to overcome the competition by process, procedure, and productivity (Krafcik, 1988). The human factor was still present, but the system itself was the foundation. In the 1990s, organizations optimized processes used technology to overhaul already efficient means and instead of just processes of individual aspects of the organization the organizations themselves became mechanisms efficient machines. The 2000s brought a renewed emphasis on data, especially big data (Bollier, 2010) and now, in 2020, we find ourselves staring yet again into a renewed call to emphasize the human factor.

Organizations have come full circle in many ways. At one time, the organization had to focus on people, not process, because the organization was people. You needed people, not automation, to complete a task, lead, delegate, and create. On this side of organizational development though, we find that managers and leaders are more in tune with people-understanding (Grunberg, McManigle, & Barry, 2020). While our technology now is unmatched compared to any other time in human history, administrators recognize that without their employees, efforts for maximum efficiency may be futile.

Even though management theories approached the organization as a system for many years, some process to be mastered, the reality is the organization has always been about people. It was never enough to simply assume Employee X and Employee Y, to hearken back to McGregor, could be ignored. Instead, Employee X and Employee Y need to be led to be managed. We believe, in order to effectively engage employees, organizations should consider the implications and development of communication systems. If the organization *is* people, then the organization survives because of communication. Organizations must come to an understanding of how employees, supervisors, and systems engage. That engagement can in part be identified as a communication phenomenon.

Communication in organizations will be approached more thoroughly in Chapter 3. As a preface, communication in many ways is the organization. Without appropriate communication systems, both internal and external, the organization will struggle to survive. It is important, then, for organizations to focus on communication efficiency, efficacy, and effectiveness (Pirjol & Radomir, 2017). In many ways, communication has become a defining and differentiating factor of the 21st century organization. Communication has changed rapidly, obviously since the 1960s when McGregor positioned his Theory X and Theory Y, but even more recently with the advent of instant messaging platforms, like Slack, as well as true remote work. The organization today looks drastically different even compared to the "typical" organization of 2010.

1.2 The 21st Century Organization

At the time of this writing, 2020–2021, the main and consistent constant of organizations is change and in many cases rapid change. Organizations on a regular basis deal with new technology, globalization, and new regulations (Lartey, 2020). In addition, organizations have had to deal with ever-changing crisis situations in 2020, such as a global pandemic, international economic recession, and societal unrest in the United States. These realities are hard to overcome and only enhance organizational complexity. In essence, industries are forms of chaos and thus chaotic systems (Lartey, 2020).

However, even in the midst of sustained chaos, these organizational systems can evolve, grow, and adapt. It is important, though, to recognize the internal audiences and different perceptions and perspectives of employees in order to thrive in today's chaos-filled climate. While communication remains important in all organizations, the manifestations of how communication in organizations are implemented, and the relationships with supervisors/employees should be a continual area of study.

Communication infiltrates all areas of organizational operations. For our purposes, we address communication and organizational implications from a variety of topics and perspectives. In analyzing the 21st century organization, it is crucial to approach a few topics that underscore the importance of how communication impacts the organizational structure and, more specifically, relationships or perceptions within organizations across the generational spectrum. To reiterate, for this reason, this book addresses the following organizational variables: the job search, organizational culture, organizational identification, mentorship and supportive workplace communication, dissent and conflict, workplace satisfaction, and remote or virtual work.

Connecting Organizational Variables to the 21st Century Workplace

The 21st century organization is a multifaceted organism. From job search to retirement, employees, and their managers, generally navigate an ever-changing, fast-paced environment where expectations change constantly. Our economy has shifted, generally, from one focused on manual labor and commodities to a knowledge-driven repository centered on human capital (Dede, 2010). This reality, in addition to the ever-changing ways employees complete their work tasks, at the moment the explosion of remote or virtual work, makes organizational study a fascinating area of study. We realize that the journey an employee takes from becoming an employee to completing their work as a valuable member of the organization will look different depending on the industry. However, there are general components that apply to almost all organizations – in some capacity. For one, the ever-increasing demand for specific job-related skills continues to become more prominent (Van Laar, Van Deursen, Van Dijk, & De Haan 2017). In addition, the job search process in general, for new employees, and especially younger employees, those of the Millennial or Generation Z affiliation, can be particularly stressful (Wanberg, Ali, & Csillag, 2020). The job search also sets the stage for success of both the organization and the employee (van Hooft, Krammeyer-Mueller, Wanberg, Kanfer, & Basburg, 2020).

The culture of the organization is not only a major factor in the actual job search process, as employees strive to find the proper 'fit', but also directly impacts both the productivity and lifespan of the organization itself (Roulin & Krings, 2020). Organizational culture, then, becomes the catalyst and foundation for future success. The culture comprises several different components but, as they relate to the actual employee, how the individual identifies with the organization (Bavik, 2016), communication, both positive and negative (Gochhayat, Giri, & Suar, 2017), in the organization, and workplace or job satisfaction (Meng & Berger, 2019), should be considered as key organizational determinants. We believe a data-driven understanding of generational differences, relating to these workplace-specific variables, can help us understand the 21st century organization in a new and unique way. In the sections that follow, our generational study is described and we briefly position some of our main findings.

1.3 The Generational Study

Throughout this book data will be presented from a comprehensive generational study. The main goal of the study was to better understand the multi-generational workforce. Therefore, the study was designed as a detailed and in-depth online survey, including both open- and close-ended questions.

Following institutional research protocol approvals at two universities, participants were solicited using Amazon M-Turk so that a sample of people throughout the United States could be utilized. To be eligible to participate, participants needed to be at least 18 years of age and currently working full-time in the United States. There were no restrictions about industry, education level, or other demographics. Participants were paid one dollar upon completion of the survey. Participants (N = 339) were also recruited from a large, public university in the Mid-Atlantic United States. Student participants received course research credit for completing the survey.

In all, completed surveys from 1,148 participants were analyzed. An additional 16 completed surveys were not included in the analysis, as they were completed by self-identified members of "The Silent Generation" or "Generation Z." Table 1.1 below contains demographic breakdowns for all participants, and by each of the three generations explored in this text: Baby Boomers (born 1946–1964), Generation X (born 1965–1981), and Millennials (born 1982–1999).

As Table 1.1 demonstrates, a range of length of experience in the workplace, as well as industries employed in range across all three groups. Perhaps not surprisingly, older generations report longer time spent in their current position, on average, as compared to younger generations. We see the highest education level attainment in Gen X, and the lowest among Millennials, likely an effect of recruiting current university students. Participants were asked to identify one of 35 options of the industry in which they were employed. The most common industries represented in the sample are Healthcare/ Medicine and Education. The sample is somewhat more white (78.4%) and female (61.8%) than a truly representative sample of the United States is, but a representation of different races and ethnic groups is apparent.

The online survey was a total of 77 questions including 52 closed-ended, Likert-style questions, and 25 open-ended response questions. Participants first confirmed that they were working full-time before consenting to the study and then self-selecting their generational membership. The survey measures are listed below, followed by Table 1.2, which provide reliability coefficients for each scale and subscale used, as well as means and standard deviations for each.

Organizational Communication Scale (Roberts & O'Reilly, 1974). A series of 22 questions to determine how people communicate at work. Participants were instructed to imagine a typical week at work and answer the questions accordingly. Some of the questions in this measure included yes/no answer choices, filling in percentages of time spent equaling 100%, multiple choice, and Likert scale responses.

Job Searching. A combination of Likert-style questions and short answer questions were used to determine job searching strategies, expectations, and experiences. Questions determined the extent to which the job search was easier or harder than participants expected, how they responded to violated job searching expectations, and how much time they spent job searching as reflecting on their most recent job search.

Organizational Culture Survey (Glaser, Zamanou, & Hacker, 1987). A total of 36 questions to determine the extent to which the following organizational culture statements applied to participants, answered

Table 1.1 The Survey and Measures

Demographics	All N = 1148	Baby Boomers N = 93	Gen X N = 234	Millennials N = 821
Sex				
Female	61.8% (N = 709)	65.6% (N = 61)	58.1% (N = 136)	62.4% (N = 512)
Male	38.1% (N = 437)	33.3% (N = 31)	41.9% (N = 98)	37.5% (N = 308)
Race				
White	78.4% (N = 900)	82.8% (N = 77)	78.2% (N = 183)	78% (N = 640)
Black	6.2% (N = 71)	7.5% (N = 7)	6.4% (N = 15)	6% (N = 49)
Latino(a)	4.5% (N = 52)	1.1% (N = 1)	4.3% (N = 10)	5% (N = 41)
Asian	7.6% (N = 87)	4.3% (N = 4)	8.1% (N = 19)	7.8% (N = 64)
American Indian/ Alaskan Native	1.1% (N = 13)	2.2% (N = 2)	.4% (N = 1)	1.2% (N = 10)
Native Hawaiian/ Pacific Islander	.2% (N = 2)	—	—	.2% (N = 2)
Other/Mixed Race	2% (N = 23)	2.2% (N = 2)	2.6% (N = 6)	1.8% (N = 15)
Education Level				
High School	36.2% (N = 416)	21.5% (N = 20)	15% (N = 35)	44% (N = 361)
Associate's degree	15.1% (N = 173)	17.2% (N = 16)	15.8% (N = 37)	14.6% (N = 120)
Bachelor's degree	33.3% (N = 382)	34.4% (N = 32)	43.6% (N = 102)	30.2% (N = 248)
Master's degree	12.2% (N = 140)	21.5% (N = 20)	22.6% (N = 53)	8.2% (N = 67)
Doctoral degree	3.2% (N = 37)	5.4% (N = 5)	3% (N = 7)	3% (N = 25)

(Continued)

Table 1.1 (Continued)

Demographics	All N = 1148	Baby Boomers N = 93	Gen X N = 234	Millennials N = 821
Time in Current Position				
In years	M = 4.53 (SD = 5.25)	M = 10.76 (SD = 8.24)	M = 8.04 (SD = 6.52)	M = 2.82 (SD = 2.83)
Range	.08–40 years	.33–40 years	.08–25 years	.08–22 years
Top Industries Employed In:	41.6% employed in top 5 Industries	65.6% employed in top 5 Industries	49.6% employed in top 5 Industries	41.% employed in top 5 Industries
	1. 10.8% Healthcare/ Medical	1. 21.5% Healthcare/ Medical	1. 13.7% Education	1. 11% Food Service
	2. 10.1% Education	2. 17.2% Education	2. 9.4% Healthcare/ Medicine	2. 10% Healthcare/ Medical
	3. 8.7% Food Service	3. 8.6% Finance/ Banking/ Insurance	3. 8.5% Government/ Military	3. 8.3% Education
	4. 6.5% Retail	4. 7.5% Manufacturing	4. 6% (each) Manufacturing/ Retail	4. 7.2% Retail
	5. 5.5% Finance/ Banking/ Insurance	5. 5.4 % (each) Government/ Military and Non-Profits	4. 6% Finance/ Banking/ Insurance	5. 5% Finance/ Banking/ Insurance

Table 1.2 Reliability Coefficients, Means, and Standard Deviations for All Study Scales and Subscales

Scale	Subscales	Alpha	Mean (SD)
Mentoring and Communication Social Support Scale *5-point scale*		.891	3.67(.69)
	Career Mentoring	.811	3.58(.90)
	Coaching	.683	3.32(.94)
	Collegial – Social	.826	3.69(.88)
	Collegial – Task	.855	4.01(.81)
Organizational Communication Conflict Instrument *7-point scale*		.831	4.09(.63)
	Non-confrontation strategies	.870	3.97(1.13)
	Solutions-oriented strategies	.874	4.77(.94)
	Control strategies	.820	3.25(1.13)
Organizational Culture Survey *5-point scale*		.973	3.57(.79)
	Teamwork	.921	3.60(.80)
	Morale	.933	3.57(.95)
	Information Flow	.822	3.51(.88)
	Involvement	.887	3.38(1.00)
	Supervision	.922	3.66(.91)
	Meetings	.891	3.33(.94)
Organizational Identification Scale *7-point scale*		.943	3.76(1.24)
Organizational Assimilation Index *5-point scale*		.938	3.80(.74)
	Supervisor Familiarity	.851	3.76(.98)
	Acculturation	.888	4.18(.84)
	Recognition	.926	3.86(1.01)
	Involvement	.881	3.43(1.05)
	Job Competency	.725	3.89(.80)
	Role Negotiation	.780	3.71(1.00)
Organizational Dissent Scale *5-point scale*		.824	3.02(.60)
	Articulated Dissent	.826	3.25(.77)
	Latent Dissent	.862	2.78(.83)
Job Satisfaction *5-point scale*		.893	3.76(1.06)
Communication Satisfaction *5-point scale*		.966	3.78(.82)
	Personal Feedback	.924	3.65(1.01)
	Organizational Identification	.873	3.85(.89)
	Communication Climate	.908	3.61(1.00)
	Horizontal Communication	.818	3.83(.77)
	Relationship with Supervisor	.924	3.97(.96)

using a five-point Likert-style scale where one was "to a little extent" and five was "to a very great extent." Questions included items such as: "People I work with function as a team," "This organization respects its workers," and "Job requirements are made clear by my supervisor." The scale can be examined via one overall dimension, as well as along six sub-dimensions: Teamwork, morale, information flow, involvement, supervision, and meetings.

Organizational Identification Scale (Cheney, 1983). This unidimensional scale instructed participants to think of their role as an employee within their organization and selected the answer that best represented their attitude toward their organization, using a Likert scale. The measure is a total of 25 questions on a 7-point Likert scale, including items such as: "I find it easy to identify with my organization," "I feel that my organization cares about me," and "I am glad I chose to work for my organization rather than another company."

Organizational Assimilation Index (Meyers & Oetzel, 2003). A series of 20 questions about how participants feel part of their organization answered on a five-point Likert-style scale where one indicates "strongly disagree" and five indicates "strongly agree." Items included statements such as "I understand the standards of the company," "I know the values of my organization," and "I feel involved with this organization." This scale contains six subdimensions: supervisor familiarity, acculturation, recognition, involvement, job competency, and role negotiation.

Mentoring and Communication Support Scale (Hill, Bahniuk, Dobos, & Rouner, 1989). A total of 15 questions on a 5-point Likert-type scale where five indicates "strongly agree" and one indicates "strongly disagree." Questions included items such as "Someone of higher rank frequently devotes extra time and consideration to me," "I have had an associate teach me the informal rules of my organization," and "my associates and I are friends as well as coworkers." This scale contains four subscales: Career mentoring, coaching, collegial – social, and collegial – task. The coaching subscale was the only scale or subscale to fall just short of the widely recognized .70 criteria for assessing a scale's reliability. Means across the overall scale and subscales were well over the midpoint, ranging from $M = 3.32$ for coaching to 4.01 for collegial-task.

Organizational Communication Conflict Instrument (Putnam & Wilson, 1982). A total of 30 questions were answered on a 7-point Likert scale to assess how often participants engage in each of the behaviors described. Questions included items such as: "I blend my ideas with others to create new alternatives for resolving a conflict," "I steer clear of disagreeable situations," and "I argue insistently for my stance." The instrument includes three subdimensions for how individuals deal with conflict: nonconfrontation strategies, solution-oriented strategies, and control strategies.

Organizational Dissent Scale (Kassing, 2000a). A series of 18 statements about how people express their concerns about work answered using a five-point Likert-style scale where one indicates "strongly disagree" and five indicates "strongly agree." Items included statements such as "I complain about things in my organization with other employees," "I share my criticism of the organization openly," and "I speak with my supervisor or someone in management when I question workplace decisions." The scale contains two sub-scales: Articulated dissent and latent dissent.

Job Satisfaction Scale (Pond & Geyer, 1991). Six statements answered using a five-point Likert-style scale to determine a person's level of job satisfaction. Statements including things like "Knowing what I know now, if I had to decide all over again, I would still take this job," and "This job compares with my ideal job."

Communication Satisfaction Scale (Downs & Hazen, 1977). A total of 25 questions answered on a 5-point Likert scale to determine overall communication satisfaction in the workplace, by examining five subdimensions: personal feedback, organizational identification, communication climate, horizontal communication, and relationship with supervisor.

Table 1.3 presents a correlation matrix of all major scales presented in this text. The largest correlations seen are positive ones between *Communication Satisfaction* and several other scales, including: Organizational Culture, Organizational Assimilation, and Job Satisfaction. While those correlations are some of the highest, these four scales all share significant, positive, moderate-to-large relationships. Mentoring and communication Support, along with Organizational Identification also share significant, positive, but slightly smaller correlations with most of the variables previously discussed.

Some logical negative relationships are also apparent. The dark side of organizational communication: Measures of Conflict and Dissent interestingly share no relationship with one another, but demonstrate small, negative relationships with Mentoring and Social Support, Organizational Identification (Conflict) and Organizational Assimilation (Dissent).

Table 1.3 Correlations Between Eight Major Study Scales

	1.	2.	3.	4.	5.	6.	7.
1. Organizational Culture Survey							
2. Organizational Identification Scale	-.264**						
3. Organizational Assimilation Index	.632**	-.306**					
4. Mentoring and Communication Support Scale	.390**	-.200**	.496**				
5. Organizational Communication Conflict Instrument	-.045	-.137**	.010	.135**			
6. Organizational Dissent Scale	-.037	-.012	.121***	.141**	-.013		
7. Job Satisfaction Scale	.634**	-.294**	.567***	.328**	-.048	-.092**	
8. Communication Satisfaction Scale	.776***	-.298**	.733**	.436**	.001	-.014	.695**

1.4 Conclusion

This volume approaches an organizational study from a generational perspective. To do so, the authors provide substantial data reflective of the variables mentioned above and subsequently use previous literature to provide a context for generational differences and implications of these generations in the workplace. The next chapter explores the multigenerational workplace in more depth.

References

Arghode, V., Jandu, N., & McLean, G. N. (2020). Exploring the connection between organizations and organisms in dealing with change. *European Journal of Training and Development*. Advance online publication. http://dx.doi.org/10.1108/EJTD-06-2020-0095

Bavik, A. (2016). Identification of organizational culture in the hospitality industry. *Tourism and Hospitality Management, 12*, 197–210. https://doi.org/10.1108/S1871-317320160000012015

Bollier, D. (2010). *The promise and peril of big data*. The Aspen Institute.

Cheney, G. (1983). On the various and changing meanings of organizational membership: Field study of organizational identification. *Communication Monographs, 50*, 342–362.

Dede, C. (2010). Comparing frameworks for 21st century skills. In J. Bellanca & R. Brandt (Eds.), *21st century skills* (pp. 51–76). Solution Tree Press.

Downs, C., & Hazen, M. (1977). A factor analysis of communication satisfaction. *Journal of Business Communication, 14*, 63–74.

Glaser, S. R., Zamanou, S., & Hacker, K. (1987). Measuring and interpreting organizational culture. *Management Communication Quarterly, 1*, 173–198.

Gochhayat, J., Giri, V. N., & Suar, D. (2017). Influence of organizational culture on organizational effectiveness: The mediating role of organizational communication. *Global Business Review, 18*, 691–702. https://doi.org/10.1177%2F0972150917692185

Grunberg, N. E., McManigle, J. E., & Barry, E. S. (2020). Using social psychology principles to develop emotionally intelligent healthcare leaders. *Frontiers in Psychology, 11*. https://doi.org/10.3389/fpsyg.2020.01917

Hill, S. E., Bahniuk, M. H., Dobos, J., & Rouner, D. (1989). Mentoring and other communication support in the academic setting. *Group and Organization Studies, 14*, 355–368.

Kassing, J. W. (2000a). Investigating the relationship between superior-subordinate relationship quality and employee dissent. *Communication Research Reports, 17*, 58–70.

Krafcik, J. F. (1988). Triumph of the lean production system. *Sloan Management Review, 30*, 41–52. https://search.proquest.com/docview/224963951?accountid=10003

Lartey, F. M. (2020). Chaos, complexity, and contingency theories: A comparative analysis and application to the 21st century organization. *Journal of Business Administration Research, 9*, 44–51. doi: 10.5430/jbar.v9n1p44

McGregor, D. (1960). *The human side of enterprise*. McGraw-Hill.

Meng, J., & Berger, B. K. (2019). The impact of organizational culture and leadership performance on PR professionals' job satisfaction: Testing the joint mediating effects of engagement and trust. *Public Relations Review, 45*, 64–75. https://doi.org/10.1016/j.pubrev.2018.11.002

Meyers, K. K., & Oetzel, J. G. (2003). Exploring the dimensions of organizational assimilation; Creating and validating a measure. *Communication Quarterly, 51*, 438–457.

Pirjol, F., & Radomir, L. L. (2017). The role of internal communication on the efficiency of the activity in an organization. *Business Excellence and Management, 2*, 27–45.

Pond, S., & Geyer, P. (1991). Differences in the relation between job satisfaction and perceived work alternatives among older and younger blue-collar workers. *Journal of Vocational Behavior, 39*, 251–262.

Putnam, L. L., & Wilson, C. E. (1982). Communicative strategies in organizational conflicts: Reliability and validity of a measurement scale. *Communication Yearbook, 6*, 629–652.

Roberts, K. H., & O'Reilly, C. A. (1974). Measuring organizational communication. *Journal of Applied Psychology, 59*, 321–326.

Roulin, N., & Krings, F. (2020). Faking to fit in: Applicants' response strategies to match organizational culture. *Journal of Applied Psychology, 105*, 130–145. https://doi.org/10.1037/apl0000431

Stait, N. (1972). Management training and the smaller company: SWOT analysis. *Industrial and Organizational Training, 4*, 325–330. https://doi.org/10.1108/eb003232

van Hooft, E. A. J., Kammeyer-Mueller, J. D., Wanberg, C. R., Kanfer, R., & Basbug, G. (2020). Job search and employment success: A quantitative review and future research agenda. *Journal of Applied Psychology*. Advance online publication. https://doi.org/10.1037/apl0000675

Van Laar, E., Van Deursen, A. J. A. M., Van Dijk, J. A. G. M., De Haan, J. (2017). The relation between 21st-century skills and digital skills: A systematic literature review. *Computers in Human Behavior, 72*, 577–588. https://doi.org/10.1016/j.chb.2017.03.010

Wanberg, C. R., Ali, A. A., & Csillag, B. (2020). Job seeking: The process and experience of looking for a job. *Annual Review of Organizational Psychology and Organizational Behavior, 7*, 315–317. https://doi.org/10.1146/annurev-orgpsych-012119-044939

2   A Generational Perspective

The multigenerational workplace has become an area of fascinating study. While not a novel concept, generational differences became a mainstream area of study in 1991 with the creation of Generational Theory (otherwise known as Fourth Turning Theory) by Strauss and Howe. They assume that generations are cyclical and that a generation lasts around 20–22 years. Within this 20–22 era, life experiences become unifying and identifying categories for members of a particular era. Despite some conflicting reports regarding the rigor of generational theory (Jones, 1992), it has become a helpful categorization tool to engage personnel differences in the modern workplace.

2.1 An Overview of the Multigenerational Workplace

We are in the midst of a generational revolution. As a matter of identification, cultural identity, an individual's sense of self-derived group membership (Jameson, 2007), has become intricately tied – in some circles – to generational affiliation. Schullery (2013) defined a generation as those born between a specified year range and who share life experiences. We will go into more detail about this below. As a cultural identity, generational alignment may have a significant impact on workplace practices, organizational culture, and workplace communication.

The multigenerational workplace has become an area of fascinating study. While not a novel concept, generational differences became a mainstream area of study in 1991 with the creation of Generational Theory (otherwise known as Fourth Turning Theory) by Strauss and Howe. They assume that generations are cyclical and that a generation lasts around 20–22 years. Within this 20–22 era, life experiences become unifying and identifying categories for members of a particular era. Despite some conflicting reports regarding the rigor of generational theory (Jones, 1992), it has become a helpful categorization tool to engage personnel differences in the modern workplace.

Again, Schullery (2013) argues that a generation consists of those born between a specified year range who share certain, major, life experiences relating to pop culture, economic conditions, natural disasters, and more. Strauss and Howe (1991) added that generations are also defined by similarities in values, affections, and beliefs. No matter the actual life stage or year distinction of generations, members of a generational cohort are examined together because of shared interests and experiences.

Workplaces tend to, rightly, distinguish among generations. Organizations should understand generational differences in order to effectively manage staff and attract new talent while retaining valuable employees (Chenkovich & Cates, 2016; Lyons & Kuron, 2014). It is true that generational differences manifest uniquely in the workplace, partly because of the influence of other generations on those who may be older or younger. Millennials, for instance, have long been known as a cohort that craves clarity of expectation and efficient workplace communication (Watkins & Smith, 2019). The desire for efficiency is just one example of a generational difference that becomes a generational marker. However, there are other unique generational traits that impact the workplace positively and negatively.

Unfortunately, differences between generations have created unprecedented and unforeseen conflicts in the workplace (Bright, 2010). To achieve maximum workplace effectiveness or, at the very least, adapt to changing workplace demographics, academicians must continue to study generational distinctions. In addition, because of the vital nature of communication to, and within, the organization, we must consider how generational distinction impacts perceptions of communication within organizations.

The workplace, though, is not just an exhibition of generational differences. Widespread academic foci have been placed on generational differences in the workplace, but it is also important for organizations to consider generational similarities (Costanza & Finkelstein, 2015). Broadly, Mencl and Lester (2014) found that generations were similar on 7 of the 10 work values examined. A clear understanding of generational similarities in the workplace can help supervisors establish an organizational culture and communication infrastructure that is truly cross generational and effective for the majority of employees.

Ultimately, we know that all generations desire "meaningful work, professional development and advancement opportunities, a positive work-life balance" (Strawser, Coffey, & Martin, 2019, p. 188) and an organizational identity that reinforces autonomy and individuality. These tried and true employee preferences transcend-specific age categories and serve as foundational pillars that corporations can use to enhance a multigenerational workplace. As such, it is important to continually assess how generational culture can create more dynamic organizations.

Recently, Millennials became the largest generation in the workplace, and in some avenues, work environments can contain five generations: Traditionalists, Baby Boomers, Generation X, Millennials, and Generation Z/iGen. While the core desires of each generation are relatively similar, contrary to popular belief, the way younger generations communicate their expectations are different. Below, a brief summary of each generation is provided, but these will be expanded throughout this text.

Traditionalists (Born pre-1945)

This demographic, otherwise known as the Silent Generation, arrived at the tail end of the "Greatest Generation." Most were born as the Great Depression and WWII were dying down. Members of this group are rule followers. They are more conservative, traditional, respectful, and sacrificial work, for most Traditionalists, is an opportunity to earn money crucial for survival (Beekman, 2011). Traditionalists, like Boomers after them, appreciated the hierarchical structure of the "typical" organization. Cates, Cojanu, and Pettine (2013) believe formality should be a defining factor of an organization's culture when managing traditional workers. Traditionalists prefer a more controlled leadership style and, compared to other generations, appreciate individual work and work assignments (Hammill, 2005). Traditionalists are still present in some organizations but primarily have moved into retirement.

Baby Boomers (Born 1946–1964)

Depending on the source, Baby Boomers are considered workaholics, materialistic, and greedy (Crampton & Hodge, 2007; Gibson, Greenwood, & Murphy Jr., 2009). In addition, Boomers tend to gravitate toward the concept of the "American Dream" and have (or have had) issues with work/life balance. They are also responsible, exceptionally loyal to their children, and ambitious. Like Millennials, Boomers are sometimes viewed as entitled (Lyons, 2005) and somewhat self-absorbed (Weil, 2008). Boomers are still prominent in organizations, although more are leaving the workforce.

Generation X (1965–1980)

Members of Gen X are small in number compared to their pre-decessors and successors. They are rebellious. They saw their parents work, constantly, and wanted more balance. Gen Xers revel in pessimism. They are skeptical, cynical, and suspicious. An oft-forgotten group today, at one time, like Millennials, members of Generation X were discussed and criticized in popular literature (Pekala, 2001). Because many of them grew up in homes where parents both worked (Hart, 2006), Generation Xers had to grow up quickly and become more independent (Yahr & Schimmel, 2013). In terms of sheer numbers, there are fewer Generation Xers compared to their bookend generations, Boomers and Millennials.

Millennials (1981–1996)

Probably to the relief of Generation X, at the arrival of their work-place transition, Millennials become the primary generational fodder for criticism and study. Stereotypes for this group typically include entitled, perfectionist, achievement-oriented, tolerant, confident, tech-savvy, unfocused, "me"-first, etc. Millennials have grown up in a world of constant advocacy. Rarely did they have to fight for themselves because others, specifically their parents, fought for them. Millennials may not have workplace expectations that are drastically different from their predecessors, but they do express their expectations a little differently (Martin, 2005). This particular generation has a strong desire for technology-infused work, especially related to remote or flexible work situations, and they value a positive work climate and culture (Shaw & Ogilvie, 2010; Sutcliffe & Dhakal, 2018). As they navigate their professional path, professional development is important for this group because they want to move up the corporate ladder quickly (Ng & Feldman, 2010).

Generation Z/iGen (1997–2012)

Generation Z grew up in a digital world. Even more than Millennials, they are digital natives and digital enthusiasts. They tend to have a risk-averse existence. This group is entrepreneurial, image-driven, and focused on their personal "brand," and they are deeply connected to their values and social causes. In terms of numbers, Generation Z members comprise 32% of the global population. Often, Generation Z will consider their jobs, job security, and job fit as matters of utmost importance (Bernier, 2015). Z's are incredibly diverse and open-minded (Pew Research Center, 2014), well-connected (Shatto & Erwin, 2016), and, unfortunately, have a shortened attention span (Hallowell & Ratery, 2010). While it is beneficial to focus on generational similarities as well as differences, a baseline understanding of different generations is important as organizations work with members of each generation individually and collectively.

2.2 Historical Development of Generational Differences

One of the biggest antecedents to generational differences is the external environment where people grow up and the happenings of the world that influence daily life. For instance, Baby Boomers were influenced by the Civil Rights Movement, the Cold War, and the sexual revolution, while Generation X lived through an energy crisis, Desert Storm, Watergate and the women's liberation. Millennials have been greatly affected by world events such as 9/11 and various school shootings, as well as a polarizing and unprecedented political environment. The era in which generations grow up greatly affects their core values surrounding things like education, which Millennials see as a major financial expense and burden, but which Boomers internalize as a birthright. Core values also include preferred methods of communication, with the younger generations utilizing technology more than any previous generation; money and financial habits; family values and systems; and overall cultural outlook. Taking the historical context of each generation into consideration helps to define the unique attributes of every cohort.

In the workplace, history is a major indicator of generational differences used to help explain variables such as work/life balance, job expectations, work ethic, rewards and compensation, retention, and retirement, to name a few. Perhaps most important to realize is that in the sense of generational differences, history does not repeat itself. Meaning, organizations cannot look to previous generations to help predict and understand how up and coming generational cohorts will behave in the workplace. This is why it is imperative to study each generation separately, but also collectively, as this volume does.

2.3 Development of Multigenerational Understanding

It is well documented that these generations are, to say the least, different. Boomers, for instance, are career loyalists, while Millennials typically transition jobs, or even careers, more often (Strawser et al.,

2019). Members of Generation X are more balanced in their workplace expectations but, unlike their Millennial coworkers they tend to appreciate individual, not collaborative work (Strawser et al., 2019). Those in Generation Z are pragmatic, and not very idealistic. There is also a widespread acknowledgment that their tech reliance may be causing mental instability (Twenge, 2017).

Even in terms of communication, each generation has different preferences. Boomers tend to rely on phone calls or face-to-face meetings; Generation X members will balance their operations between face-to-face and tech-driven means; and Millennials and iGen workers appreciate digital communication, although members of Gen Z are on record saying they enjoy face-to-face methods as well (Patel, 2017). These communication differences are extremely important to consider as organizations develop operations and procedures. And, in essence, these elements can help build or destroy organizational culture and communication.

To develop a multigenerational understanding of the workplace, empirical data are continuously needed. It is important for academicians to consider implications of varying generations on all facets of the organization. Throughout this volume, we will be synthesizing relevant empirical literature and supplementing that with our own findings from a comprehensive multigenerational study of workplace communication.

It is par for the course for each generation to be negatively stereotyped in the media, which carries over into the workplace and interpersonal relationships. Eventually, as the next generation begins to develop and influence trends, attention is diverted to the newest cohort. To date, empirical research has focused on examining how generations communicate in interpersonal relationships; health contexts; families; in groups and teams; in the classroom; and within the workplace. However, a limited amount of research examines how generations work together. This has created a communication divide that further segregates and stereotypes generations rather than contributing to holistic and inclusive communication practices. As workplaces make efforts to increase diversity and inclusion, generational cohort should remain a top priority. It is through the multigenerational workplace that people learn from one another through mentorships, observation, and shared experiences.

2.4 Conclusion

Academic study of the workplace must be continuously refined. While it is important to understand the organization at large, we believe a thorough understanding of communication in the workplace will help us have a greater understanding of expectations and effectiveness. As a lens to study communication in the workplace, generational differences present an applicable and popular dimension as different eras collide in an environment centered on outcomes. The next chapter will further explore communication in the workplace and communication preferences of different generations based on previous literature.

References

Beekman, T. (2011). Fill in the generation gap. *Strategic Finance*, 15–17.

Bernier, L. (2015). *Getting ready for Gen Z. Canadian HR Reporter, 28*, 11–16.

Bright, L. (2010). Why age matters in the work preferences of public employees: A comparison of three age-related explanations. *Public Personnel Management, 39*, 1–14.

Cates, S. V., Cojanu, K. A., & Pettine, S. (2013). Can you lead effectively? An analysis of the leadership styles of four generations of American employees. *International Review of Management and Business Research, 2*, 1025–1041.

Chenkovich, K., & Cates, S. (2016). Welcome to the Millennial generation: Should this generation be attracted, managed and retained by corporations differently? *International Journal of Management and Human Resources, 4*, 79–93.

Costanza, D. P., & Finkelstein, L. M. (2015). Generationally based differences in the workplace: Is there a there there? *Industrial and Organizational Psychology, 8*, 308–323. https://doi.org/10.1017/iop.2015.15

Crampton, S. M., & Hodge, J. W. (2007). Generations in the workplace: Understanding age diversity. *The Business Review, 9*, 16–23.

Gibson, J. W., Greenwood, R. A., & Murphy, E. F., Jr. (2009). Generational differences in the workplace: Personal values, behaviors, and popular beliefs. *Journal of Diversity Management, 4*, 1–8.

Hallowell, E., & Ratery, J. (2010). *Driven to distraction*. Anchor Books.

Hammill, G. (2005). "Mixing and managing four generations of employees." FDU Magazine Online. Retrieved September 1, 2009, from www.fdu.edu/newspubs/magazine/05ws/generations.htm.

Hart, K.A. (2006). *Generations in the workplace: Finding common ground. Lab Management, 38*, 26–27.

Jameson, D. A. (2007). Conceptualizing cultural identity and its role in intercultural business communication. *Journal of Business Communication, 44(3)*, 199–235.

Jones, G. L. (1992). Strauss, William and Neil Howe 'Generations: The History of America's Future, 1584–2069'. *Perspectives on Political Science, 21(4)*, 218.

Lyons, S. (2005). Are gender differences in basic human values a generational phenomenon? *Sex Roles: A Journal of Research, 53*, 763–778. Retrieved from http://wwwfindarticles.com/p/articles/mi_m2294/is_9–10_53/ai_n16084047/print

Lyons, S., & Kuron, L. (2014). Generational differences in the workplace: A review of the evidence and directions for future research. *Journal of Organizational Behavior, 35*(S1), S139–S157. https://doi.org/10.1002/job.1913

Martin, Carolyn A. (2005). From high maintenance to high productivity. *Industrial and Commercial Training, 37*, 39–44. doi:10.1108/00197850510699965.

Mencl, J., & Lester, S. W. (2014). More alike than different: What generations value and how the values affect employee workplace perceptions. *Journal of Leadership & Organizational Studies, 21*, 257–272. https://doi.org/10.1177/1548051814529825

Ng, T. W., & Feldman, D. C. (2010). The relationships of age with job attitudes: A meta-analysis. *Personnel Psychology, 63*, 677–718. doi:10.1111/j.1744-6570.2010.01184.x.

Patel, D. (2017). 8 ways generation Z will differ from millennials in the workplace. Retrieved from https://www.forbes.com/sites/deeppatel/2017/09/21/8-ways-generation-z-will-differ-from-millennials-in-the-workplace/#7220595776e5

Pekala, N. (2001). Conquering the generational divide. *Journal of Property Management, 66*, 30–38.

Pew Research Center (2014). *Millennials in adulthood. Detached from institutions, networked with friends.* Retrieved from http://www.pewsocialtrends.org/2014

Schullery, N. M. (2013). Workplace engagement and generational differences in values. *Business Communication Quarterly, 76*, 252–265.

Shatto, B., & Erwin, K. (2016). Moving on from millennials: Preparing for Generation Z. Journal of *Continuing Education in Nursing, 47*, 253–254. doi:10.3928/00220124-20160518-05

Shaw, S., & Ogilvie, C. (2010). Making a virtue out of a necessity: Part time work as a site for undergraduate work-based learning. *Journal of European Industrial Training, 34*, 805–821. doi:10.1108/03090591011080986.

Strauss, W., & Howe, N. (1991). *Generations: The history of America's future, 1584–2069.* William Morrow and Company.

Strawser, M. G., Coffey, L., & Martin, J. (2019). Millennial cultural transitions: Higher education experience as an expectation for workplace culture. In M. Z. Ashlock & A. Atay (Eds.), *Examining millennials reshaping organizational cultures: From theory to practice* (pp. 175–192). Lexington Books.

Sutcliffe, J. E., & Dhakal, S. P. (2018). Youth unemployment amidst aged care workers shortages in Australia. *Equality, Diversity and Inclusion: An International Journal, 37*(2), 182–198. doi:10.1108/edi-05-2017-0105.

Twenge, J. (2017) *iGen: Why today's super-connected kids are growing up less rebellious, more tolerant, less happy and completely unprepared for adulthood.* Atria Books.

Watkins, B., & Smith, S. A. (2019). Best practices for communicating work-place culture on social media. In S. A. Smith (Ed.), *Recruitment, retention, and engagement of a millennial workforce* (pp. 37–48). Lexington Books.

Weil, N. (2008). Welcome to the generation wars: As Boomer bosses relinquish the reins of leadership to Generation X both are worrying about Generation Y. For the good of the enterprise, everyone needs to do a better job of getting along. *CIO, 21.* https://www.cio.com/article/2437236/gen-y--gen-x-and-the-baby-boomers--workplace-generation-wars.html

Yahr, M.A., & Schimmel, K. (2013). Comparing current students to a pre-millennial generation: Are they really different?. *Research in Higher Education Journal, 20,* 1–8. doi:doi.org/10.1097/00006216-200101000-00005.

3 Understanding Generational Communication Differences in the Workplace

This chapter provides a contextual overview of internal communication efforts and internal communication effectiveness specifically from a multigenerational perspective. Best practices for internal communication are provided.

3.1 An Overview of Internal Communication

Internal communication should promote communication effectiveness among people within an organization. Different mechanisms can be used to promote and stimulate internal communication, and some of those will be discussed here. But, generally, effective internal communication is integral to organizational success (Welch & Jackson, 2007) leading to high social capital (Lee, 2009) and higher levels of workplace performance and customer service (Tourish & Hargie, 2009). Clampitt and Downs (1993) report that effective communication, stemming from audits, can improve productivity, reduce absenteeism, create higher quality products and service, increase motivation and innovation, and reduce costs. Communication within the organization cannot and should not be ignored, and the actual process of internal communication, as well as varying best practices, continues to be a more popular area of study (Corcic, Vokic, & Vercic, 2020).

Historically, internal communication research stems from organizational communication (Jablin & Putnam, 2001) as well as organizational psychology (Lowenberg & Conrad, 1998). In 2005, Kalla identified four internal communication domains: business communication (communication skills of employees), management communication (management skills and capabilities for communication), corporate communication (formal communication), and organizational communication (philosophical issues related to the organization's communication). These dimensions are helpful for recognizing the multifaceted nature of internal communication; however, categorizing how internal communication manifests in organizations does not take into consideration employee communication preferences.

Employers and supervisors should continue to explore internal communication study for many reasons especially because of how it relates to engagement. Schaufeli and Bakker (2004) posit that engagement has three components: vigor, dedication, and absorption. These three categories are helpful in identifying employees who are invested in their work, show a sense of pride in their work, and fully concentrated and happy at work. Engagement and communication are complementary factors. We know that internal communication strategies influence employee engagement (Karanges, Johnston, Beatson, & Lings, 2015). Employee engagement is important for several reasons, including enhancing supportive or positive communication and reducing employee turnover (Kang & Sung, 2017). Especially important to millennials, internal communication can also help promote transparency between employees and supervisors (Men, O'Neil, & Ewing, 2020; Mishra, Boynton, & Mishra, 2014). These factors can enhance overall organizational climate and culture and can help employees feel more connected to the organization, often leaving employees better informed. As organizations strive to help employees understand expectations and overall operations, clarity of message, frequency, and format must be approached in a way that is employee friendly.

Within organizations, actual internal communication platforms have evolved. Recently, beyond more traditional channels, some organizations have intentionally sought to increase employee engagement and communication tactics through social media (Ewing, Men, and O'Neil 2019). Globally, digital tools, obviously, have grown in scope throughout organizations (Akhmetshin, Kulibanova, Ilyina, & Teor, 2020). Communication tools, and internal communication strategies, have been used for project management as well as corporate messages (Qatawneh, 2018). The uses, structure, and range of internal communication strategies and tools or platforms to communicate internally continue to become more efficient and, if used properly, more effective.

To assess internal communication, practitioners will often use communication audit principles. Communication audits do just what the name implies; they take an overarching audit of the communication practices of an organization to determine if the communication practices are working. Typically, audits involve an assessment of internal communication, but clients and other external stakeholders can also be involved. A communication audit is useful in multiple ways. For one, it helps organizations determine communication strengths and weaknesses.

Clarity of messaging, both internal and external, can also be evaluated. If your goal is external, an audit allows you to identify the opinions of your customers and the success of media messaging and/or public relations efforts holistically. Finally, communication audits help supervisors, managers, and C-suite executives determine if communication efforts are aligned with the mission, vision, and strategic plan of the organization. Audits are not a central focus of this chapter, but it is important for context to understand that there are ways to measure internal communication and satisfaction of employees related to their communication preferences and expectations.

Employee preferences should be understood in order to create more intentional internal messages. And, even more so, we need to understand different communication preferences as they correlate to generational identification. Employees have different communication needs (Ruck & Welch, 2012). However, more research is required regarding what employees desire and what they believe is important in the internal communication process (Uusi-Rauva & Nurkka, 2010). Thankfully, generational differences may provide a framework for understanding employee communication preferences.

3.2 Communication Effectiveness in a Multigenerational Workplace

Communication preferences in the workplace tend to see incredible variety based on generational differences. Pollak (2019) posits that the two primary communication differences among generations in the workplace are communication style preferences and a perceived difficulty communicating with those outside one's own generation. This reality manifests itself in the workplace through potential conflict or bitterness, and a lack of productivity may result. To ensure workplace operations are as efficient as possible, communication format and frequency must be generation-spectrum friendly. There is not one single style of communication that will work for all employees equally, but there are certain principles that resonate in the multigenerational workplace.

First, it is important to note that a divergence exists in how communication preferences are reported in the workplace, and some sources minimize generational differences. While there is a variance in preference between generations, these variances may not be that pronounced (Woodward & Vongswasdi, 2016). Messaging truths like simplicity and clarity transcend age. Instead, the variance seems to occur in the strength of individual preferences and the expectations of immediacy and source (Hall, 2016). And, probably of even more importance, the manager or supervisor can influence job satisfaction and productivity by practicing more competent communication (Madlock, 2008).

Competency, then, must be adapted to the receiver. Millennials, for instance, prefer workplace communication that is more positive, frequent, and open (Chou, 2012). Millennials also crave very specific expectations and direct communication (Ferri-Reed, 2014). These preferences, along with feedback that tends to skew more supportive, are hallmark desires of millennial employees. Certainly, these desires, according to the research, are millennial-centric, but employees generally want communication to be positive, direct, frequent, and specific (Pollak, 2019). Baby Boomers and Gen Xers, though, unlike Millennials and Generation Z, demand less transparency of their supervisors (Stewart, Oliver, Cravens, & Oishi, 2017). Generally, too, members of Generation X tend to vocalize their concerns to supervisors and coworkers more consistently compared to Millennials, who often rely on text-based communication to air grievances or seek clarification (Stewart et al., 2017). The reliance on technology for messaging also continues to evolve as each new generation becomes more prominent in the workplace. Compared to older generations, for instance, Gen Zers tend to rely more on technology for routine communication (Schroth, 2019).

These communication preferences will differ in intensity depending on the organizational culture and the type of vocation. However, the ability of managers to adapt to their individual workers and respect differing opinions based on feedback, transparency, criticism, or the use of technology to spread messages, can be a differentiating factor for more effective and productive workplace communication. All told, supervisors and managers should be ready to adapt and must exhibit communication competence.

3.3 Developing an Internal Communication Strategy

Employees within organizations are currently overwhelmed with information. Therefore, internal communication strategies need to be strategic and work together, rather than compete for the employees' attention. To do that, an understanding of the different sources of internal communication is necessary. The three most common sources are hierarchical, mass media, and social media/networks (Whitworth, 2011). Hierarchical sources include people such as CEO's, presidents, vice presidents, managers, directors, supervisors, and anyone who has a role with authority over others in the organization (Whitworth, 2011). Mass media sources refer to internal communications that reach broad audiences (such as the entire organization) through mediums like email blasts, newsletters, videos, blogs, etc. Finally, social media/networks include websites, such as internal portals that are similar to social media websites; social media websites such as LinkedIn and Facebook; and the informal communication networks that exist between employees, like Slack and text messaging (Whitworth, 2011). The best internal communication strategies use all of these sources to help maximize the effectiveness of sharing information with employees to further improve communication satisfaction and engagement, which has strong correlations to employee retention.

Hierarchical communication is the most traditional form of internal communication and is still one of the most frequently applied strategies. However, some managers more effectively share information than others, and sometimes, sharing information becomes a game of telephone where the messages get warped and lost in translation down the chain. Therefore, while managers should continue to be a leading source in internal communication strategies, they should also be used to direct people to the information, such as on an internal organizational portal, so that employees are free to read, interpret, and save the information themselves without the reliance on their manager. In this sense, when developing internal communication strategies, the hierarchical structure present in organizations should operate as directors of information and encourage employees to seek out information.

When sharing information with employees, a source for additional questions should always be provided. In some instances, employees should be directed to their managers, while in others, employees should be encouraged to talk with human resources, product development, and/or facilities for more information. This helps create a two-way street of information sharing, which according to Grunig's Excellence Theory, is the most effective way to share information (Gillis & IABC, 2011). When a two-way dialogue is present, the organization moves closer to fulfilling its goals (Whitworth, 2011).

The best internal communication strategies mirror the broad range of mass media available to employees outside of the workplace and integrate the technological evolutions that have infiltrated our daily lives. Furthermore, the strongest internal communication strategies share both good and bad news with honesty and transparency (Whitworth, 2011). Millennials, particularly, expect fully transparent communication from the organizations they choose to work for, so providing this information through publications like newsletters, organizational magazines, and/or featured blog posts gives employees the option to consume this content. This is complementary to information that *must* be shared such as policy changes and updates, which are better shared through email, hierarchical communication, and on internal portal announcements. This demonstrates one of the major points for successful internal communication: channels should work together rather than compete for attention.

Another important consideration when developing an internal communication strategy is inclusion among a diverse workforce. A multigenerational workforce counts as diversity and requires the same attention as other factors of diversity. According to Roberson (2006), "diversity focuses on organizational demography, whereas inclusion focuses on the removal of obstacles to the full participation and contribution of employees in organizations" (p. 217). This is another reason why using a multipronged approach to internal communication (hierarchical, mass media, social media/networks) is vital when developing an internal communication strategy. Through our understanding of generational communication preferences, we know that generational membership influences communication preferences. Therefore, providing the opportunities to receive information from interpersonal sources (hierarchical, social networks), from technology (social media, mass media), and on-demand when it is most convenient for the receiver (mass media) are important considerations that only a multipronged internal communication strategy can provide.

A final consideration is to be strategic in creating the internal communication strategy to motivate people to use all channels and mediums available, which can be done by creating exclusive content for each outlet and refraining from repeating content across multiple platforms, as suggested by Whitworth (2011).

3.4 Exploring and Evaluating Communication in the Workplace

One way to measure communication in the workplace is through the use of the Organizational Communication Scale, OCS, originally developed by Roberts and O' Reilly (1974). Their scale, which does exhibit some reliability and validity concerns, explores workplace communication through varying dimensions from an employee perspective. Some concerns surround low reliability on several subscales, as well as several one-to-two item subscales. These dimensions include trust in supervisor, influence of superior, importance of upward mobility, desire for interaction, accuracy (of coworkers at different levels), summarization, gatekeeping, overload, directionality of information, and degree of satisfaction with communication.

Three of the concepts the OCS measures: trust in supervisor, perceived influence of supervisor, and desire for upward mobility in one's organization are thought to not directly measure communication per se, but related concepts. We examine generational differences among these first.

All three subscales, or sub-dimensions, are measured on 7-point Likert scales and coded such that greater numbers indicate greater endorsement of the subscale (i.e. greater perceived influence). Across all participants, the subscales of Trust in Supervisor (3 items; $M = .53$, $SD = 1.11$, alpha $= .739$) and perceived Influence of Supervisor (2 items; $M = 4.94$, $SD = 1.39$, alpha $= .730$) reached acceptable reliability, although perceived Importance of Mobility in one's organization ($M = 4.87$, $SD = 1.69$, alpha $= .687$) fell just shy of the traditional .700 cutoff. An ANOVA was utilized to examine significant differences among the generational groups on these three subscales and data are presented below in Table 3.1.

As the table demonstrates, there were no significant differences in trust in supervisor or perceptions of their influence. There were, however, significant and moderate-to-large size differences among each of the generational groups and how important they rated their chance for upward mobility in their organization. Here, Millennials rated mobility the most important, followed by Gen X and lastly Baby Boomers. This finding may be due in part to age and time to move upward in an organization.

There are three measures in the Organizational Communication Scale which ask participants to estimate how much time they spend communicating with supervisors, subordinates, and peers, respectively, so that the total number would be equal to 100%. These questions asked about the frequency of interacting with each of the three groups, the total time spent *receiving* information from each group, and the

Table 3.1 Generational Differences in Trust in Supervisor, Influence of Supervisor, and Mobility from the Organizational Communication Scale

OCS Sub-scale	Baby Boomers M(SD)	Gen X M(SD)	Millennials M(SD)	F (2, 1147)	eta^2
Trust in Supervisor	4.63(1.25)	4.52(1.21)	4.53(1.06)	.444	.00
Influence of Supervisor	4.90(1.48)	4.82(1.50)	4.98(1.35)	1.189	.00
Importance of Own Mobility	**3.79(1.82)**[a]	**4.64(1.80)**[b]	**5.07(1.59)**[c]	27.983**	.05

**$p < .001$, *$p < .05$.
[a,b]Significant differences between groups as determined by Tukey HSD post hocs. Scores that significantly differ from the other two scores are bolded.

total time spent *sending* information to each group. A related, yet distinct item asked about the time spent communicating across modalities – including in writing, face-to-face, or via telephone. These descriptive statistics and significance testing for differences across groups are presented below in Table 3.2.

In terms of overall time spent interacting with others in the workplace, we see that all three generations report about the same amount of time interacting with their superiors – between 25 and 30% of all interactions. Differences here lie with Millennials, who spend about 10% more time interacting with peers, and about 10% less time spent interacting with subordinates. Millennials are less likely to be working with subordinates in general. Time spent interacting with others is very similar across Baby Boomers and Gen X, a pattern we see in many of the other time spent-related data.

The data on time spent receiving and sending information to superiors, subordinates, and peers demonstrate that Gen X spends significantly less time receiving *and* sending information to their superiors. They spend significantly more time sending and receiving information with subordinates when compared to Millennials.

Millennials also demonstrated significant differences in the frequency of communicating across modalities, including written communications, face-to-face communication, and communication via telephone. They report spending significantly more time communicating face-to-face and less time communicating via writing compared to Baby Boomers and Gen X, who did not differ in time spent communicating via different modalities. This may be because of the types of industries each group is employed in. As reviewed in chapter 1, Millennials are more likely to be in retail and food service industries, where face-to-face communication is paramount.

The last dimension of perceptions about workplace communication from the OCS examined here is the reported desirability of frequently interacting with one's superiors, subordinates, and peers. Results of the three ANOVAs are presented below in Table 3.3.

Where greater numbers indicate less desirability in interacting with each co-worker group, we see small, yet significant differences related to superiors, subordinates, and peers. Gen X is the outlier in two of the three groups, and Millennials the outlier in one. The data reveal that Gen X participants desired *less* interaction with their supervisors, and *more* interaction with their peers, as compared to both Baby Boomers and Millennials. Interestingly, the group less likely to have subordinates, Millennials, indicated a significant *less* desire to interact with subordinates.

Table 3.2 Generational Differences in Time Spent Communicating with Supervisors, Subordinates, and Peers

		Baby Boomers M percent	Gen X M percent	Millennials M percent	F (2, 1147)	eta²
Time spent: *Interacting* with:	Supervisors	25.53%	27.38%	30.41%	**3.660***	**.01**
	Subordinates	26.48%ᵃ	26.98%ᵃ	**16.83%ᵇ**	**20.875****	**.04**
	Peers	47.98%ᵃ	45.64%ᵃ	**52.75%ᵇ**	**6.925****	.01
Time spent *Receiving* Information from:	Supervisors	47.49%ᵃ	**44.88%ᵇ**	53.56%ᵃ	**10.390****	**.02**
	Subordinates	18.60%ᵃ	19.93%ᵃ	**11.86%ᵇ**	**18.390****	**.03**
	Peers	33.90%	35.19%	34.58%	.906	.00
Time spent *Sending* Information to:	Supervisors	42.96%ᵃ	**38.10%ᵇ**	44.39%ᵃ	**4.471***	**.01**
	Subordinates	23.99%ᵃ	23.53%ᵃ	**16.52%ᵇ**	**10.810****	**.02**
	Peers	33.32%	37.98%	37.74%	1.124	.00
Time spent communicating via:	Writing	29.94%ᵃ	26.47%ᵃ	**22.50%ᵇ**	**5.992**	**.01**
	Face-to-face	52.38ᵃ	52.71ᵃ	**59.61%ᵇ**	**7.104**	**.01**
	Telephone	16.04%	17.14%	15.32%	1.142	.00

$**p < .001$, $*p < .05$.
[a,b]Significant differences between groups as determined by Tukey HSD post hocs. Scores which significantly differ from the other two scores are bolded.

Table 3.3 Generational Differences in Desirability of Frequent Interaction with Supervisors, Subordinates, and Peers

		Baby Boomers M (SD)	Gen X M (SD)	Millennials M (SD)	F (2, 1147)	eta^2
Desirability of Frequently Interaction with: (*Where greater numbers reflect less desirability on a 7-point scale*)	Supervisors	3.12(1.66)	**3.54(1.79)**[a]	3.22(1.71)[a]	**3.725***	**.01**
	Subordinates	3.40(1.91)[a]	3.38(1.97)[a]	**3.81(2.01)**[b]	5.254	**.04**
	Peers	2.75(1.63)[a]	**3.07(1.61)**[b]	2.83(1.58)[a]	**3.611***	.01

**p < .001, *p < .05.

[a,b]Significant differences between groups as determined by Tukey HSD post hocs. Scores that significantly differ from the other two scores are bolded.

3.5 Best Practices for Establishing Effective Internal Communication

As managers and supervisors attempt to lead a multigenerational workplace, they should not overlook the importance of communication. There are different best practices that can be used to enhance internal communication, no matter the organization.

Best Practice 1: ACORN Your Organization

In 2008, Tolbize identified ACORN imperatives as methods to aid intergenerational comfort. These imperatives include accommodating employee differences by learning about their unique needs and serving them accordingly, creating workplace choices such as allowing the workplace to shape itself around the work being done, and operating from a sophisticated management style which would involve adapting leadership style to context or balancing concerns for tasks and concerns for people. This acronym is a helpful reminder for organizations. Generally, supervisors, managers, and leaders must adapt to the changing organization and changing employees.

Best Practice 2: Create Multimodal Communication Channels

Organizations, when attempting to develop internal communication strategies that resonate across the generational spectrum, should use different platforms that can be easily adapted to the organization's culture and communication structure. Creating multimodal messages, meaning messages across a variety of channels and platforms, can help reach a wide range of internal audiences.

Best Practice 3: Develop an Internal Communication Strategy

Strategic communication planning is important. Do not assume that all employees will respond the same to every message. Instead, think broadly about how communication fits into the broader organizational structure and consider developing an actual internal communication strategy that fits your organizational ethos. Your strategy should include all three of the internal sources: hierarchical, mass media, and social media/networks.

Best Practice 4: Audit, Analyze, and Adjust

Every six months, the internal communication team should conduct an audit of internal communications to determine what went out, what it said, how often it was sent, how it was sent, and how it was received. This requires forethought in the creation of the internal communication strategy to construct internal communications that are measurable and trackable. For instance, tracking the open rates of internal email announcements is a great metric. Doing an audit will give organizations a larger overview to analyze what is working and what is not so that they can eliminate the strategies that are not providing a return. From this data, organizations can adjust their internal communication strategies accordingly, which in many cases, does not require more communication but instead less communication that is more strategic and informative.

3.6 Conclusion

This chapter and the corresponding data from our study showcase the importance of prioritizing internal communication, especially with a multigenerational workforce. Sharing the same message in multiple ways is important to ensure that it is received and transmitted accurately, taking into consideration the different ways that employees prefer to communicate. As the chapters that follow will demonstrate, effective internal communication can have implications for communication satisfaction, support, conflict, leadership, and job satisfaction.

References

Akhmetshin, E. M., Kulibanova, V. V., Ilyina, I. A., & Teor, T. R. (2020). Innovative internal communications tools and their role in fostering ethical organization behavior. *2020 IEEE Communication Strategies in Digital Society Seminar*, 75–81. doi: 10.1109/ComSDS49898.2020.9101245.

Chou, S. Y. (2012). Millennials in the workplace: A conceptual analysis of millennials' leadership and followership styles. *International Journal of Human Resource Studies*, 2, 71–83. doi: 10.5296/ijhrs.v2i2.1568

Clampitt, P. G., & Downs, C. W. (1993). Employee perceptions of the relationship between communication and productivity: A field study. *The Journal of Business Communication*, 30, 5–29.

Corcic, D. S., Vokic, N. P., & Vercic, A. T. (2020). Does good internal communication enhance life satisfaction? *Journal of Communication Management*, 4, 1–14. https://doi.org/10.1108/JCOM-11-2019-0146

Ewing, M., Men, L. R., & O'Neil, J. (2019). Using social media to engage employees: Insights from internal communication managers. *International Journal of Strategic Communication*, 13, 110–132. https://doi.org/10.1080/1553118X.2019.1575830

Ferri-Reed, J. (2014). Are millennial employees changing how managers manage? *The Journal for Quality & Participation*, 37, 15–35.

Gillis, T., & IABC (2011). *The IABC handbook of organizational communication: A guide to internal communication, public relations, marketing, and leadership.* John Wiley & Sons.

Hall, A. (2016). Exploring the workplace communication preferences of millennials. *Journal of Organizational Culture, Communications and Conflict, 20,* 35–44.

Jablin, F. M., & Putnam, L. L. (2001). *The new handbook of organizational communication.* Sage.

Kalla, H. K. (2005). Integrated internal communications: A multidisciplinary perspective. *Corporate Communication, 10,* 302–314.

Kang, M., & Sung, M. (2017). How symmetrical employee communication leads to employee engagement and positive employee communication behaviors: The mediation of employee-organization relationships. *Journal of Communication Management, 21,* 82–102. doi: 10.1108/JCOM-04-2016-0026

Karanges, E., Johnston, K., Beatson, A., & Lings, I. (2015). The influence of internal communication on employee engagement: A pilot study. *Public Relations Review, 41,* 129–131. https://doi.org/10.1016/j.pubrev.2014.12.003

Lee, R. (2009). Social capital and business management: Setting a research agenda. *International Journal of Management Reviews, 11,* 247–273.

Lowenberg, G., & Conrad, K. A. (1998). *Current perspectives in industrial/organizational psychology.* Allyn & Bacon.

Madlock, P. (2008). The link between leadership style, communicator competence, and employee satisfaction. *Journal of Business Communication, 45,* 61–78. doi: 10.1177/0021943607309351

Men, L. R., O'Neil, J., & Ewing, M. (2020). Examining the effects of internal social media usage on employee engagement. *Public Relations Review, 46,* 1–9. https://doi.org/10.1016/j.pubrev.2020.101880

Mishra, K., Boynton, L., & Mishra, A. (2014). Driving employee engagement: The expanded role of internal communications. *International Journal of Business Communication, 51,* 183–202. https://doi.org/10.1177%2F2329488414525399

Pollak, L. (2019). *The remix: How to lead and succeed in the multigenerational workplace.* Harper Business.

Qatawneh, H. (2018). Hybrid communication strategies and tools as a strategic lever to improve supply chain performance. *International Journal of Business Management, 13,* 181–187. https://doi.org/10.5539/ijbm.v13n3p181

Roberts, K. H., & O' Reilly, C. A. (1974). Measuring organizational communication. *Journal of Applied Psychology, 59,* 321–326.

Roberson, Q. M. (2006). Disentangling the meanings of diversity and inclusion in organizations. *Group & Organization Management, 31,* 212–236.

Ruck, K., & Welch, M. (2012). Valuing internal communication; management and employee perspectives. *Public Relations Review, 38,* 294–302. https://doi.org/10.1016/j.pubrev.2011.12.016

Schaufeli, W. B., & Bakker, A. B. (2004). Job demands, job resources, and their relationship with burnout and engagement: A multi-sample study. *Journal of Organizational Behavior, 25,* 293–315. doi:10.1002/job.248

Schroth, H. (2019). Are you ready for Gen Z in the workplace? *California Management Review, 61*, 5–18. https://doi.org/10.1177%2F0008125619841006

Stewart, J. S., Oliver, E. G., Cravens, K. S., & Oishi, S. (2017). Managing millennials: Embracing generational differences. *Business Horizons, 60*, 45–54. https://doi.org/10.1016/j.bushor.2016.08.011

Tourish, D., & Hargie, O. (2009). Communication and organizational success. In O. Hargie & D. Tourish (Eds.), *Auditing organisational communication: A handbook of research, theory, and practice* (2nd ed., pp. 3–26). Routledge.

Tolbize, A. (2008). Generational differences in the workplace. University of Minnesota. *Research and Training Center on Community Living*. Retrieved from https://rtc.umn.edu/docs/2_18_Gen_diff_workplace.pdf

Uusi-Rauva, C., & Nurkka, J. (2010). Effective internal environment-related communication: An employee perspective. *Corporate Communications: An International Journal, 15*, 299–314.

Welch, M., & Jackson, P. R. (2007). Rethinking internal communication: A stakeholder approach. *Corporate Communications: An International Journal, 12*, 177–198. https://doi.org/10.1108/13563280710744847

Whitworth, B. (2011). Internal communication. In T. Gillis (Ed.), *The IABC handbook of organizational communication* (2nd ed., pp. 195–206). Jossey-Bass.

Woodward, I. C., & Vongswasdi, P. (2016). More that unifies than divides: Intergenerational communication preferences in the workplace. *Communication Research and Practice, 3*, 358–385. https://doi.org/10.1080/22041451.2017.1275259

4 Generational Expectations of the Job Search

This chapter will serve as a precursor to the subsequent chapter on organizational culture. Specifically, this chapter will focus on not only the recruitment of employees from the organizational perspective but also how the idea that different generations have different job searching strategies and expectations. In order to recruit and retain, organizations need to be aware of and initiate talent.

4.1 The Evolving Job Search Process

The job search is an inherently communicative process that involves looking for new work, which has become a common activity in today's economy, regardless of current employment status (Wanberg, Basbug, vanHooft, & Samtani, 2012). Securing employment is directly linked to both the job search behaviors that a job seeker performs and the amount of effort a job seeker exerts during their job search (Blau, 1993). Traditionally, job searching research has focused on the process as a coping mechanism to deal with the stressful experience of losing a job (DeFrank & Ivancevich, 1986; Leana & Feldman, 1988). As research in this area has evolved and expanded, it has shifted to focus on job search predictors and outcomes, including the effect that communication has on job searching activity (Doyle, 2014; Gordon, 2010; Holmstrom, Clare, & Russell, 2014; Holmstrom, Russell, & Clare, 2013; Piercy & Lee, 2018; Smith, 2017; Wanberg et al., 2012).

Job searching is a difficult task that "requires the use of complex strategies, substantial self-control, and self-regulation skill" (Price & Vinokur, 1995, p. 192). Job searching has also been defined as "the outcome of a dynamic, recursive, self-regulated process" (Kanfer, Wanberg, & Kantrowitz, 2001, p. 838). Similarly, job searching behavior refers to the specific activities that an individual engages in to acquire knowledge about employment opportunities (Bretz, Boudreau, & Judge, 1994). Job searching behaviors include preparatory efforts such as gathering information and securing leads, as well as active behaviors like applying to jobs and interviewing (Bretz et al., 1994). Empirically, job searching effectiveness has been measured based on the number of job offers received (Saks & Ashforth, 2000).

Research contributing to job searching has focused on three main areas: intensity-effort, content-direction, and temporal-persistence, with most research emphasizing the intensity-effort dimension (Wanberg et al., 2012). For example, people who spend more time job searching tend to find jobs quicker. Several variables have been attributed to this finding such as perceived control, employment commitment, social support, age, gender, and education (Kanfer et al., 2001). Individual differences may help understand the different communication strategies used for job searching. A personality and job searching meta-analysis demonstrated that high levels of extraversion and conscientiousness were positively and significantly related to job searching, such that people higher in those two personality characteristics had better job search outcomes (Kanfer et al., 2001). Further, those with proactive personalities have shorter and more successful job searches (Brown, Cober, Kane, Levy, & Shalhoop, 2006). It has also been reported that when job seekers receive helpful and supportive messages from others relating to their job search, their intensity of job searching increases (Holmstrom et al., 2013).

There are a number of ways to search for a job, some of which are influenced by generational membership. Undoubtedly, the changes in technology paired with the generational cohort have greatly influenced how people find jobs and create their career expectations. People can job search using a number of channels such as websites, recruiters, a personal network, advertisements, and word-of-mouth. Granovetter (1995) outlined three basic techniques people use to search for jobs: formal means, personal contacts, and direct application. Formal means include using sources such as advertisements and employment agencies. The defining characteristics of job searching through formal means is that the job seekers use the sources of an impartial intermediary to find prospective employers. In contrast, job searching through personal contacts relies on the help of an individual whom the job seeker knows personally is personally known by the job seeker in a context unrelated to job searching, such as a friend or family member. Through a reliance on an interpersonal network, the job seeker is better able to connect and communicate with potential employers and have the opportunity to speak directly with decision makers (Mau & Kopischke, 2001). Finally, direct application techniques describe how a job seeker may contact a potential employer directly (online, via phone, or in person), does not rely on an intermediary of any source (partial or impartial), and has not learned of the opportunity through an interpersonal relationship. It is reported that among all job seekers, regardless of age and/or experience, at least 60% of jobs are found through networking or personal connections, and that using a strategy of networking can result in faster employment than formal methods of job searching (Doyle, 2014; Granovetter, 1995). Gordon (2010) found that approximately 46% of job seekers made a direct application to the employer before getting hired.

Job seekers that use multiple methods for job searching have shorter and more successful job searches, regardless of the amount of time spent job searching, which aligns with the intensity effort dimension of job searching previously discussed. To that end, most job seekers use more than one strategy for job searching, which typically includes involves a primary strategy and a secondary strategy. Furthermore, research findings suggest that using the internet for job searching along with other sources such as personal requests, can lead to faster job attainment (Kuhn & Mansour, 2014; Stevenson, 2009). Undoubtedly, online sources have changed how people search and apply for jobs. The Pew Research Center reports that among job seekers in the last few years, regardless of age and experience, the most frequently used and most important source for job searching was online information (Smith, 2015). Conversely, previous research indicates that older people tend to use fewer social resources (such as social networking websites like Facebook and LinkedIn) for job searching. This begs the question: how do people of different generations search for jobs?

4.2 Generational Differences and in Job Search Strategies

Previous research has helped to demonstrate the generational differences that are present in job searching, and the qualitative data of our study continues and expands this area of inquiry. However, job searching strategies could have more to do with amount of experience, which is only tangentially related to generational membership. Nonetheless, because we now have a multigenerational workforce, it is helpful to understand how people at different stages of their career, which currently corresponds to generational membership, search for employment.

The following data illustrate how each generation present in the workforce searches for a job. These data were both quantitatively and qualitatively collected using open-ended survey responses. Collectively, it helps to understand which job searching strategies are the most often used by each generation, which has implications for recruiting a multigenerational workforce.

Job Searching Strategies

All of the participants in this study (N = 1,148) indicated that they used more than one job searching strategy, regardless of generational membership. The following table indicates the most popular job searching strategies used by each generation (Table 4.1).

These data indicate that when it comes to searching for a job, generational membership makes a minimal difference, which is helpful for organizations to understand. The direct application strategy was the most common, primary job searching strategy for all three generations represented in this study. Job searching through aggregate websites like Indeed.com, Monster, and Career Builder was the second most common strategy used by all cohorts. The secondary strategy used by all cohorts is personal networking, but as the data indicate, it is used by fewer people than direct application and websites for job searching.

Generational membership makes the greatest difference with regard to the job search when examining the use of social media. Millennials noted the highest use of social media for job searching, including websites such as Facebook and LinkedIn, which both offer features to post available opportunities and apply directly through the social networking websites. The data show that as age increases, the use of social media for job searching decreases. This is particularly interesting given the fact that Gen X and Baby Boomers are some of the heaviest users of social media sites like Twitter and Facebook. However, these data illustrate that Gen X and Baby Boomers use social media primarily for reasons beyond outside job searching and do not consider social media when looking for a job, despite their recreational and non-professional use of the sites.

Table 4.1 Generational Differences of Job Search Strategies

Generation	Direct Application	Websites	Personal Networking	Social Media
Millennials	57.7%	55.3%	33.6%	18.3%
Gen X	58.5%	49.1%	35.5%	14.6%
Baby Boomers	30%	19.9%	18.8%	1%

4.3 Expectations of the Job Search Process

Underlying the job search are career expectations and expectations for the process and outcome of the job search. Burgoon (1978) defines expectations as a belief that something will happen, as compared to a desire for something to happen, and argues that expectations are developed through social norms. Therefore, a career expectation is a belief that something is going to or likely to happen with regard to career-related issues, such as finding a job, and may be formed in part based on the social norms established within each generation. For example, Ng, Schweitzer, and Lyons (2010) discovered that Millennial job seekers (under age 30) have realistic expectations about their first job and salary, but unrealistic expectations about rapid advancement opportunities and a fulfilling life outside of work.

Expectations are based on social norms, and we use them as filters for planning and executing our communication. Norms help people enter job interviews with a handshake rather than a hug and help people form their expectations about situations, particularly in professional contexts. While norms are one of the largest antecedents to expectations, people also form expectations based on a combination of other sources (Smith, 2017). For instance, when it comes to job searching and career development, the mass media is influential in the formation of expectations. When people hear and read reports in the news about the economy and the labor market, they adjust their own expectations accordingly. People also form their expectations based on the stories they hear from and about others. This is one potential reason why job searching on social networking sites has increased in popularity. As we hear other people find jobs and opportunities through sites like this, we turn to the same places and expect similar, perhaps better, results for ourselves. Interpersonal sources are particularly influential when it comes to forming expectations about the duration and intensity of job searching in both positive and negative ways. Expectations are also formed through observation or social learning and direct experience. Humans inherently learn by watching and learn by doing. As people watch other members of their friends and family search for jobs and secure employment, they learn about the job searching process, which informs their own personal expectations. Similarly, if someone previously had a grueling job search that lasted months or even years, they are likely to have negative expectations about the process of finding a job, despite the other variables, like their qualifications and the economy, that can influence the process.

Our generational data help to better understand the different kinds of expectations that job seekers have, which are important for employers to understand. Through a thematic analysis of the data, the expectations break down into four main categories: time, availability, rejection, and effort. While the themes are not surprising or particularly novel at face-value, the individual insights provide exceptional richness and honesty about the job search and how each generation experiences the same process in different ways.

Time Commitment and Duration of Job Search

Job searching is a time-consuming process, as previously discussed. The participants in this study indicated that job searching took more time than they expected (see Table 4.2), with Gen X reporting with the most frequently that job searching took longer than they expected; the greatest instance of job searching being more time-consuming than expected. Conversely, just over one-third of Baby Boomers reported job searching to be more time consuming than expected, which could be explained through their cumulative experiences of job searching allowing them to set more realistic expectations about how long it takes to find a job.

Millennials reported, overwhelmingly, that job searching was a longer process than they originally anticipated, followed by Gen X and then Baby Boomers. One Millennial participant explained: "Searching for a job was hard to find something that I wanted. I put in so many apps. I really searched long and hard." Another Millennial expressed frustration with the time it takes to get interviewed saying: "The time it takes to actually get a face-to-face meeting with someone. It was frustrating to spend time having to go through all the steps and then waiting for someone to be available to talk."

Interestingly, Gen X reported that job searching was more time consuming but not as long as they expected which could indicate that

Table 4.2 Generational Differences in Time Commitment and Duration of Job Search

Generation	Time Commitment (took more time than expected)	Duration of Search (took longer than expected)
Millennials	43.6%	71.7%
Gen X	45.9%	39.3%
Baby Boomers	35.3%	35.3%

the process required greater intensity effort than they expected. One participant explained why the process was more time consuming than they expected saying: "I spent hours perfecting a resume. I carefully added all pertinent information to my resume, just to get rejected over and over." Another Gen X participant explained, "I sent out tons and tons of resumes, applied to over 60 jobs, and had to repeatedly follow up with interviewers to get a response. All of that was unexpected, I thought the process would be more consistent and systematic."

With regard to the duration of the job search, more than half of the Gen X participants were happy the job search was shorter than they anticipated. One participant explained: "It didn't take me long to be offered a position after I started the process of looking. I was offered a couple of jobs at the same time and had to decide which one to accept." Similarly, many participants remarked at how quickly a decision was made following an interview, with many mentioning they were offered the job "on the spot" following the interview.

The data for Baby Boomers were the same – those who experienced a more time-consuming job search also reported that the job search took longer than they thought, but this was not the majority of job searching Boomers, to be clear. The majority of Baby Boomers seemingly had realistic expectations about the time required to search for a job and the duration of the job search. Those who experienced a longer and more time-consuming job search than anticipated cited several reasons including the volume and intricacies of searching online, alleged age discrimination, being overqualified, and inability to stand out among applicants. As one participant explained: "Job searching is stressful these days. You rarely get the opportunity to apply in person. Everything is done online so the employer doesn't really get a good feel about a person. It can be frustrating."

Required Effort and Ease of Job Searching

The descriptive and qualitative data indicated that, overall, the job search required less effort than anticipated. However, a slight majority of participants, except for Baby Boomers, indicated that the job search was not easier than they expected, as shown in Table 4.3. It is not surprising that those with less experience job searching reported that the job search required more effort and was harder than they expected (like Millennials). It is possible that Gen X found the job search to be harder because they have perfected their skills and are searching within professional niches, which can take longer to find and have fewer opportunities.

Rejection and Disappointment

Job searching is challenging due to the overwhelming amount of rejection, disappointment, and uncertainty. However, as our findings indicate, the majority of participants had realistic expectations in this regard, and only about one-third experienced more rejection than they were expecting (see Table 4.4). Millennials, interestingly, reported higher levels of disappointment, which indicates that rejection could be tied to their self-efficacy, as supported by previous research (Holmstrom et al., 2013; Holmstrom et al., 2014; Wanberg et al., 2012).

Although the descriptive data indicate that there was less rejection and disappointment than expected, the participants were very outspoken about these two points in their open-ended, qualitative responses. If someone were to only read the qualitative data, it would be misleading, causing someone to think that job seekers experienced high levels of rejection and disappointment. For example, one Baby Boomer said: "The amount of time before a final decision was reached was longer than expected. I was accustomed to waiting a few weeks to hear if I got a job. Instead, I waited three months in many instances just to hear

Table 4.3 Generational Differences of Effort and Ease of Job Search

Generation	Required Effort (more than expected)	Ease of Search (easier than expected)
Millennials	43.0%	42.8%
Gen X	41.9%	46.2%
Baby Boomers	36.8%	57.4%

Table 4.4 Generational Differences of Nonselection Response During a Job Search

Generation	Rejection (more than expected)	Disappointment (more than expected)
Millennials	39.8%	41.6%
Gen X	39.3%	34.5%
Baby Boomers	35.3%	27.9%

I didn't get it." To further illustrate the disappointment felt, one Millennial explained: "I didn't get a reply from companies for about a month and when I did, they were mostly rejections. I almost gave up on the whole thing. I was very disappointed in myself to be honest." Finally, hundreds of participants across generations remarked about the fact that many organizations do not notify of non-selection, which leaves you uncertain and wondering about the status of your application which is "frustrating," "disappointing," and "disrespectful," according to our participants.

4.4 Responding to Expectancy Violations

Expectancy violations theory (EVT) is a communication theory that helps predict and explain how people respond to encounters and communicative situations that do not align with their expectations. You have probably been in a situation where you were either pleasantly surprised at how things unfolded – maybe a meeting you were anticipating to be contentious but it went smoothly and faster than you planned, or a situation where things went far worse than expected – like being called in for a check-in with your boss only to be laid off or let go. These are expectancy violations, and they are abundant and natural in all contexts including the workplace.

Using the framework of EVT helps to understand how people assess whether violations are positive or negative and then how they adjust their subsequent communication. When something unexpected happens, people assess the situation. Within the context of job searching, an unexpected event could be getting called for an interview with a company you were not expecting to hear from, receiving news of a rejection, and/or receiving a job offer. Afifi and Metts (1998) explain that, "any behavior that falls outside a range of expected behaviors is theorized to produce cognitive arousal and trigger an interpretation-evaluation sequence that helps individuals cope with unexpected outcomes" (p. 367).

It is during the interpretation-evaluation phase that people assign a valence to a violation. More simply, after a violation, individuals assign either a positive or negative meaning to the violation (White, 2008). While valence helps to determine the outcomes of an interaction, it is also useful in helping people determine whether it is better to do what is expected, or to deviate from the norm when responding after a violation. To do so, people consider the communicative consequences, which are best understood through the communicator reward value (Burgoon, 1993). Communicator reward value is the concept that people possess characteristics that influence the extent to which interactions with them are rewarding (Burgoon, 1993). Typically, physical attractiveness, power, and intelligence are interpreted as rewarding traits (Burgoon, 1993), and therefore, job seekers are likely to view interviewers, CEOs, and hiring managers as rewarding.

In a job searching study about Millennial, entry-level job seekers, it was found that that positive information was evaluated as rewarding, but also showcase that bad news can be evaluated positively, in contrast to what EVT predicts. Participants considered information that provided no affirming information, such as a receipt of an application, to be positive feedback, because that information made them feel secure and relieved to know their application would be reviewed. Additionally, participants noted how their expectations were positively violated when receiving bad news, like not getting a job, followed by information relating to other available opportunities. Participants evaluated these experiences positively because they expected to receive no news at all regarding their applications. Naturally, participants evaluated this information as rewarding even when it contained bad news. The most likely explanation for this finding is because even bad news from a highly rewarding source during the job search helps to reduce uncertainty. For example, some participants discussed how they were happy to know their application was no longer being considered because it reduced their uncertainty about the job (Smith, 2017).

The reward level is central when understanding how people communicatively respond to expectancy violations while job searching. EVT explains that positively valued messages from a positively regarded source are rewarding; negatively valued messages from a positively regarded source are punishing; positively valued messages from a negatively valued source are not rewarding and may even be punishing; and negatively valued messages from a negatively valued source are not punishing and may even be rewarding (Burgoon, 1993). It has been noted that when career expectations do not align with reality, job seekers experience feelings of failure and discontent (Carvajal et al., 2000), which can inhibit the continuation of their job search, illustrating the impact that expectancy violations can have on the overall process of job searching.

When responding to unexpected situations, EVT explains that the options are to compensate or reciprocate, and the decision hinges on the reward level of the violating party (i.e. a hiring manager, an interpersonal contact, etc.) and whether or not that person is increasing or decreasing communication. For example, in high-reward relationships, such as between a hiring manager and a job candidate, EVT posits that recipients will reciprocate attempts by the communicator to increase communication.

Conversely, if the hiring manager is unresponsive or no longer communicating with the job candidate, the candidate may compensate for the decrease in communication through a change in their communication strategies (see Hale & Burgoon, 1984). These changes can include modifications to how people present themselves through their application materials by providing more information and customizing each application, adding more job searching strategies following a lack of interest, and/or adjusting the amount of time spent job searching.

The multigenerational data of this study provide greater insight into how people change their job searching strategies based on their experiences throughout the process. A series of closed-ended survey questions were asked to better understand this process, quantitatively. Then, some open-ended questions were asked to determine how strategies changed following both positive and negative expectancy violations. The presentation of this data is in what follows.

Before discerning how the violation of expectations influenced job searching strategies and subsequent communication, it is important to note how many participants felt the process of job searching met their expectations. That data are presented in Table 4.5.

These data are interesting because it shows that as age increases, the likelihood of having met expectations related to job searching also increases. This creates a robust area for future inquiry to determine a potential moderator, which could be the amount of previous experience, to better understand this relationship.

Even when expectations are met overall, however, there can still be positive and negative expectancy violations throughout the process. The data in Table 4.6 indicate how people responded to positive expectancy violations by answering two questions: 1) when things happened in my job search that were better than my expectations, I maintained my strategies and 2) when things happened in my job search that were better than I expected, I slowed down my strategies.

Table 4.5 Generational Differences of Expectation Violations Related to the Job Search

Generation	Job searching met expectations
Millennials	50.0%
Gen X	67.1%
Baby Boomers	72.0%

Table 4.6 Generational Differences of Responses to Positive Expectancy Violations During the Job Search

Generation	Maintained strategies	Slowed strategies
Millennials	69.5%	37.2%
Gen X	77.7%	24.8%
Baby Boomers	70.5%	33.8%

Table 4.7 Generational Differences of Responses to Negative Expectancy Violations During the Job Search

Generation	More Time	Greater Intensity
Millennials	58.4%	59.0%
Gen X	47.5%	56.1%
Baby Boomers	55.9%	52.9%

These data show that when things are going well, people keep doing it while job searching. However, those with less job searching experience might slow down their strategies while awaiting a job offer or as they are going through an interview process, for instance.

To determine how people respond to negative expectancy violations, the following questions were asked: 1) when things happened in my job search that were worse than my expectations, I changed my strategies to spend more time looking for a job and 2) when things happened that were worse than my expectations, I used greater intensity to find a job. This data are presented in Table 4.7.

These data are interesting because intensity rises, but that does not indicate a symbiotic relationship such that when intensity increases, the amount of time spent job searching also increases. As one Gen X participant explained: "When things weren't going well, I updated my LinkedIn a ton, I put everything on there and then I read job descriptions more closely and only applied when I actually had what they wanted." As a Millennial describes, instead of spending more time job searching, they reassessed their strategies: "I didn't spend more time searching, but I did take time to really think about what I was doing and why it might not be working and then came up with a different plan. But I have friends who also just gave up entirely."

Both the positive and negative findings indicate that EVT's prediction of compensating communication and reciprocal communication transfer to job searching across generations. When things are going well, people reciprocate by continuing to do what is working. When things are not going well, people compensate through greater intensity, more time, and readjusting their strategies for finding a job, consistent with previous research findings (Smith, 2017).

4.5 Best Practices for Recruiting a Multigenerational Workforce

Collectively, the data presented in this chapter coupled with previous research help to make informed suggestions for organizations that are recruiting a multigenerational workforce. First, organizations should post available opportunities on multiple channels, using both online and offline sources, including it's own website, as many people prefer direct application. Do not forget to utilize social media for sharing available jobs particularly if the organization is looking to hire Millennials and most likely, Gen Z, as they continue to enter the workforce. Second, share all available positions with current employees, even those outside of hiring departments. As these data and previous research indicate, personal networking is a primary strategy that job seekers use. As the next chapter will discuss, securing employment through personal networking can also lead to a better cultural fit, leading to better making the retention of employees better retention. Finally, share pertinent information, such as a hiring timeline and whether or not applicants will be notified if not selected, in the job description. This can help prospective employees set more realistic expectations. When possible, also include a point of contact so that if applicants have questions, they can get in touch.

References

Afifi, W., & Metts, S. (1998). Characteristics and consequences of expectation violations in close relationships. *Journal of Social and Personal Relationships*, *15*, 365–392.

Blau, G. (1993). Further exploring the relationship between job search and voluntary individual turnover. *Personnel Psychology*, *46*, 313–330.

Bretz, R., Boudreau, J., & Judge, T. (1994). Job search behavior of employed managers. *Personnel Psychology*, *47*, 275–301.

Brown, D., Cober, R., Kane, K., Levy, P., & Shalhoop, J. (2006). Proactive personality and the successful job search: A field study with college graduates. *Journal of Applied Psychology*, *9*, 717–726.

Burgoon, J. (1978). A communication model of personal space violations:

Explication and initial test. *Human Communication Research, 4,* 129–142.

Burgoon, J. (1993). Interpersonal expectations, expectancy violations, and emotional communication. *Journal of Language and Social Psychology, 12,* 30–48.

Carvajal, M., Bendana, D., Boxorgmanesh, A., Castillo, M., Pourmasiha, K., Rao, P., & Torres, J. (2000). Gender differentials between college students' earnings expectations and the experience of recent graduates. *Economics of Education Review, 19,* 229–243.

DeFrank, R., & Ivancevich, J. (1986). Job loss: An individual review and model. *Journal of Vocational Behavior, 28,* 1–20.

Doyle, A. (2014). How to use job search networking to find a job. Retrieved from http://jobsearch.about.com/cs/networking/a/networking.htm

Gordon, J. (2010). 50 job search statistics you need to know. Retrieved from http://careerchangechallenge.com/50-job-search-statistics-you-need-to-know/

Granovetter, M. (1995). *Getting a job: A study of contacts and careers* (2nd ed.). Chicago, IL: University of Chicago Press.

Hale, J., & Burgoon, J. (1984). Models of reactions to changes in nonverbal immediacy. *Journal of Nonverbal Behavior, 8,* 287–314.

Holmstrom, A., Clare, D., & Russell, J. (2014). Problem-focused content in the job search: Two tests of the cognitive emotional theory of esteem support messages. *Human Communication Research, 40,* 161–187.

Holmstrom, A., Russell, J., & Clare, D. (2013). Esteem support messages received during the job search: A test of the CETESM. *Communication Monographs, 80,* 220–242.

Kanfer, R., Wanberg, C., & Kantrowitz, T. (2001). A personality-motivational analysis and meta-analytic review. *Journal of Applied Psychology, 86,* 837–855.

Kuhn, P., & Mansour, H. (2014). Is Internet job search still ineffective? *The Economic Journal, 124,* 1213–1233.

Leana, C., & Feldman, D. (1988). Individual responses to job loss: Perceptions, reaction, and coping behaviors. *Journal of Management, 20,* 311–342.

Mau, W., & Kopischke, A. (2001). Job search methods, job search outcomes, and job satisfaction of recent college graduates: A comparison of race and sex. *Journal of Employment Counseling, 38,* 141–149.

Ng, E., Schweitzer, L., & Lyons, S. (2010). New generation, great expectations: A field study of the millennial generation. *Journal of Business Psychology, 25,* 281–292.

Piercy, C., & Lee, S. (2018). A typology of job search sources: Exploring the changing nature of job search networks. *New Media & Society, 21,* 1173–1191.

Price, R., & Vinokur, A. (1995). Supporting career transitions in a time of organizational downsizing. In London M. (Ed.), *Employees, careers, and job creation* (pp. 191–209). San Francisco, CA: Jossey-Bass.

Saks, A., & Ashforth, B. (2000). Change in job search behaviors and employment outcomes. *Journal of Vocational Behavior, 56,* 277–287.

Smith, A. (2015). Searching for work in the digital era. Pew Research Center.

Retrieved from https://www.pewresearch.org/internet/2015/11/19/searching-for-work-in-the-digital-era/

Smith, S. A. (2017). Job searching expectations, expectancy violations, and communication strategies of recent college graduates. *Business and Professional Communication Quarterly, 80,* 296–320. DOI: 10.1177/2329490617723116

Stevenson, B. (2009). The internet and job search. In D. Autor (Ed.), *Labor market intermediation* (pp. 67–86). Chicago, IL: University of Chicago Press.

Wanberg, C., Basbug, G., vanHooft, E., & Samtani, A. (2012). Navigating the black hole: Explicating layers of job search context and adaptational responses. *Personnel Psychology, 65,* 887–926.

White, C. (2008). Expectancy violations theory and interaction adaptation theory: From expectations to adaptation. In L. Baxter & D. Braithwaite (Eds.), *Engaging Theories in Interpersonal Communication: Multiple Perspectives* (pp. 189–202). Los Angeles, CA: Sage.

5 Perspectives on Organizational Culture

The remainder of the volume hinges on this chapter as the foundational component of the workplace. Organizational culture will be defined and presented within a historical context; then the authors will reflect on their findings and connect these findings to previous literature.

5.1 Defining Organizational Culture

2020 arguably changed many personal and professional elements of the workplace. For one, suddenly, more than ever before, organizations were under attack for their values or lack thereof. As organizations learned to pivot, downsize, re-establish values, and communicate with various stakeholders, society at large was not the only group experiencing change. Organizations were under a cultural attack in many ways and were forced to reconsider all elements of the business, which collectively contribute to an organization's culture.

Organizational culture is a saturated area of study in management, business, and communication industries. Therefore, the definition of organizational culture can be complex and varied. Typically, organizational culture is defined as a set of values, beliefs, assumptions, and symbols that define the way in which a firm conducts its business (Deal & Kennedy, 1982). Organizational culture is important because it identifies the relevant employees, customers, suppliers, and competitors and defines how an organization will interact with these parties. Organizational culture has been correlated with competitive advantage (Barney, 1986), leadership (Schein, 2010), recruitment (Braddy, Meade, & Kroustalis, 2006), retention (Sheridan, 1992), and unethical behavior (Umphress, Bingham, & Mitchell, 2010), to name a few.

Organizational culture helps us understand exactly how organizations accomplish goals and fulfill their missions and purposes (Sanchez, 2011). Culture is anecdotally referred to as "the way things are done around here," similar to hearing "because I said so" from a parent while you were growing up. Organizational culture can seem arbitrary, but it is nonetheless pragmatic as defined by Trompenaars and Hampden-Turner (1997) as "the way in which a group of people solves problems and resolves dilemmas" (p. 6). Hofstede, who is often credited for his contributions to culture research and knowledge, defines organizational culture as: "...a deeply rooted value or shared norm, moral or aesthetic principles that guides action and serves as standards to evaluate one's own and others' behaviors" (1994, p. 68). Collectively, organizational culture helps define and distinguish organizations from one another through outward symbols such as branding, dress codes, and work environment, as well as less tangible variables including values, norms, and beliefs.

5.2 Organizational Culture: A Historical Perspective

It can be argued that the understanding of organizational culture emerged through the first studies about how work is conducted, often called classical management approaches. Classical management approaches represent a collection of theories that share the underlying metaphor that organizations are machines, an idea largely informed by the industrial revolution (Eisenberg, Trethewey, LeGreco, & Goodall, 2017). The earliest organizations were modeled after empires and armies. These organizations operated with a culture of rank and were informed by the Bible and proverbs that denounced laziness, celebrated struggling, and encouraged hard work. This gave way to the bureaucratic organization that is still alive and well today.

Bureaucratic organizations use a top-down approach to management (Eisenberg et al., 2017). These organizations rely on the scientific method for production to provide information to managers that is used to organize and control workers. In a bureaucratic organizational culture, employees are passive. While bureaucratic organizations are still in existence, they can be problematic cultures that lead to abuses of power and disgruntled employees. Hence, the birth of scientific management.

Scientific management cultures have managers that are purely objective, relying on defined laws, rules, and principles for operations. The intent was to create cooperation between managers and employees, but instead, the scientific management approach created greater division and birthed what we now understand as line and staff functions in the workplace. Today, organizations where the culture is management-oriented and production-centered are considered to have a scientific management culture.

Fayol (1949) then created administrative science, later known as classical management, which still informs much of our organizational operations today. Fayol's approach to management, which is the creation of culture, included the following four elements: 1) structure, 2) power, 3) reward, and 4) attitude. His approach not only includes hierarchy and centralized decision making but also began to consider the employee's feelings through reward and attitude. This recognized the power that employees have within organizations and the importance of keeping employees happy in order to retain them. Many of Fayol's principles gave way to more modern management approaches such as human resources, human relations, and Theory Y (Eisenberg et al., 2017).

Today, organizational culture remains fluid and evolving, particularly with regard to the influence of technology and the changing ways we work including time and location. Similar to Fayol, we now understand organizational culture as having four elements. The four elements are: 1) strategy, 2) structure, 3) people, and 4) processes (Sanchez, 2011). Strategy is necessary to articulate how resources will be used and applied to help fulfill the mission of an organization. The structure then determines the positioning and distribution of resources that the organization needs to carry out the strategy. People, of course, are required to execute the strategy and create and maintain the structure. Finally, processes are the ways that tasks are implemented to create the functionality of the organization. When these four elements are in balance, Sanchez (2011) argues that a harmonious organizational culture, one that is positive and supportive of the organizational mission, exists.

5.3 Previous Research and Theory

Researchers have studied organizational culture so they can better understand various components of the workplace, including leadership; recruitment and retention of employees; change management; and job satisfaction. What follows is a brief overview of the literature in each of these areas. Before diving into the empirical literature, it is important to note that organizational culture lacks a central theory, and research typically is informed by multiple theoretical perspectives that can be successfully studied with either and both qualitative and quantitative methods.

Leadership

Leadership, similar to organizational culture, is a robust area of inquiry that draws upon the knowledge of other disciplines such as psychology, sociology, anthropology, business, and communication. Leadership and culture are correlated as they relate to the workplace. A poor leader can drive employees and customers away, whereas an inspiring and motivational leader can not only retain employees but also grow the organization internally and externally. As argued by Schein (2010), leadership and culture are fundamentally intertwined in three ways: "1) [that] leaders as entrepreneurs are the main architects of culture, 2) that after cultures are formed, they influence what kind of leadership is possible, and 3) that if elements of the culture become dysfunctional, leadership can and must do something to speed up cultural change" (p. xi).

Employee Recruitment and Retention

Particularly when examining organizational culture from a generational perspective, culture operates symbiotically with employee recruitment and retention. As discussed in the previous chapter, employees have expectations about what they want from organizations. This concept has been referred to as "anticipatory socialization" in organizational literature and focuses on forming expectations among potential employees (Dubinsky, Howell, Ingram, & Bellenger, 1986). The anticipatory socialization phase of job recruitment helps establish career expectations via realism and congruence. Realism is the degree to which recruits have a complete and accurate notion of what life is really like at an organization (Dubinsky et al., 1986). Congruence is the degree to which an organization's resources and demands, as well as a job candidate's needs and skills, are compatible (Dubinsky et al., 1986). Both realism and congruence have been shown to affect job satisfaction and turnover rates, because when the career related expectations of employees are not met, they find new employment (Porter, Lawler, & Hackman, 1975). The objective of anticipatory socialization is to influence the formation of job seekers' expectations and to reduce the likelihood of unmet expectations in the future (Wanous, 1977). This relates to organizational culture because it is during the anticipatory socialization process that prospective employees learn and assess the culture of an organization and create expectations about the working environment and potential fit.

Change Management

As we have all experienced in the last few years, change is constant, rapid, and can create uncertainty among people and within organizations. As the world around us changes, organizations are forced to either keep up or shut down, so not surprisingly, organizations work hard to remain operational which creates changes in communication and culture. As Pettigrew (1985) explains, changes within an organization are a response to business and economic events based on managerial perception, choice, and action. Previous research has already demonstrated that organizational culture plays a vital role in change management (Ahmed, 1998; DeLisi, 1990; Lorenzo, 1998; Pool, 2000; Schneider & Brief, 1996; Silvester & Anderson, 1999). This research helps to understand the association between organizational culture and attitudes toward organizational change—in other words, organizations whose organizational culture is evaluated positively are more likely to have employees with positive attitudes toward organizational change (Rashid, Sambasivan, & Rahman, 2004). Similarly, a qualitative study indicated that when employees have values that are congruent with those of the organization, they react more positively to change. Furthermore, because change can be an emotional experience, when organizations treat employees with respect during a period of change, those people become more engaged with the change (Smollan & Sayers, 2009).

Job Satisfaction

Another major area of inquiry related to organizational culture is job satisfaction. It is sensible to reason that when someone is satisfied with the organizational culture, they are more likely to also be satisfied with their job. However, as research indicates, things are not always this plain and simple. Much like organizational culture, job satisfaction is a multidimensional concept that is influenced by various internal and external factors. Job satisfaction depends on many organizational variables such as size, structure, salary, working conditions, and leadership, all of which constitute organizational culture. Early research about the relationship between organizational culture and job satisfaction indicated that job satisfaction increases as people progress to higher job levels and is based on a productive working environment (Corbin, 1977; Schneider & Snyder, 1975). Later, this research was extended by Sempane Rieger and Roodt (2002) using job satisfaction as a way to predict perceptions of organizational culture. Collectively, research in the areas of job satisfaction and organizational culture remains ongoing but demonstrates that there is a relationship between the two that requires attention from organizational leaders.

5.4 Generational Perspectives on Organizational Culture

While organizational culture has been studied in various contexts as discussed, organizational culture is also influenced by generational expectations about the workplace. At least in mass media, the multigenerational workplace is often discussed, sometimes only for comedic relief, showing that Millennials never want to talk on the phone, that Boomers cannot keep up with technological advances, and that Gen X is just merely there. This section will break down the different generational perspectives about organizational culture that exist before presenting our multigenerational data about organizational culture.

Millennials

Millennials are very outspoken about their cultural desires when entering the workforce. For instance, they have inspired the inclusion of many previously unconventional concepts, such as nap pods, pet-friendly workplaces, and co-working spaces. One of the most desired variables of a Millennial-friendly organizational culture is flexibility (Rawlins, Indvik, & Johnson, 2008) and the ability to work flexible hours (Brack & Kelly, 2012). This does not imply that Millennials do not want to work, as often reported in mass media outlets, but means that Millennials want to work on their own terms, when and where they want, to accommodate their lifestyles.

Speaking of lifestyle, work/life balance is another important component of organizational culture for Millennials. This could explain why Rawlins et al. (2008) found that Millennials want to be able to manage their personal lives while at work, if needed. A workplace that has a culture of "being seen" and logging long hours regardless of actual productivity is not the right fit for this generation. In fact, it is estimated that Millennials would be willing to give up $7,600 in salary every year to work in a desired environment (Chew, 2016). This is a major shift from previous generations who viewed work as a way to live.

Millennials value several elements of organizational culture, including corporate social responsibility; diversity and inclusion; work/life balance; results-oriented discussions through feedback and growth; and purposeful engagement (Alton, 2017). Millennials want to work for organizations that share and support their own beliefs, particularly with regard to environmental and social issues. Therefore, when organizations offer corporate social responsibility programs like recycling, carpools, and available time-off to volunteer, Millennials are more likely to apply for jobs there. This is related to Millennials politically independent viewpoints, which influence their need for diversity and inclusion in the workplace. Organizations that demonstrate support for diverse groups, by supporting gay pride month or International Women's Day for instance, earn stronger recruitment and retention efforts among Millennials.

Millennials are goal-oriented, and they thrive in cultures that give feedback and promote growth. On-the-job learning opportunities, employee resource groups, and both formal and informal mentoring and evaluations are attractive to Millennials. While the list of examples could go on and on, the bigger point is that when Millennials identify with an organization's culture, they are more likely to apply for positions and remain employed there.

Generation X

After Millennials, Generation X is the second largest generation present in today's workforce. This means that they not only have a lot of control over organizational culture but also a lot of experience to determine different variables present in an ideal organizational culture. Unlike Baby Boomers, Gen X has more experience with technology in the workplace, but they still have less digital wisdom than Millennials. This is helpful because this cohort is not afraid of technological changes, especially at work, since they have experienced rapid changes throughout their lives (Allen, 2017).

Gen X'ers are known for their high-quality work output and dedication to the work itself. Their values align with the core foundation of organizational culture, which is to work toward a shared goal or mission. In the workplace, Gen X'ers make great mentors to Millennials, while also being role models as leaders and helping to shape the future leaders within the organization (Allen, 2017). These factors contribute greatly to organizational culture. Much like Millennials, Gen X also desires a flexible organizational culture and likes to have strict work-life balance boundaries. Additionally, because Gen X has faced more underemployment than Boomers and was the first generation to enter the workforce with large debts from education, they are motivated by salaries in the workplace rather than, or instead of, other perks that can be appealing to Millennials (Mulvanity, 2001). Finally, because Boomers are choosing to remain in the workforce beyond the once standard retirement age of 65, many Gen X'ers view their opportunities for advancement as grim. Therefore, many Gen X'ers make several lateral moves among organizations to soak up as much knowledge and money as they can before moving on to a new job (Mulvanity, 2001). That's why considering how organizational culture influences Gen X is important for retaining this generation.

Some of the defining workplace characteristics of Gen X'ers include the need for appreciation, development, involvement, recognition, direct communication, and sincerity (Muchnick, 1996; Raines, 1997). In order to keep Gen X'ers happy at work, there cannot be any micromanagement, and the workplace needs to feel flexible and fun to them, elements that are inherent in organizational culture. This is also a generation that is strongly against "paying their dues" and wants recognition to be based solely on merit. Due to their needs for freedom, work-life balance, and flexibility, the best organizational culture fit for Gen X'ers is one where empathy is practiced. Leadership should understand that work does not occur in a vacuum and requires support for family, health, and diversity needs.

Baby Boomers

One of the biggest concerns and points of interest with Baby Boomers in the workplace is their use of technology. It is a misconception that Boomers are unable or unwilling to learn and adapt to new technologies. The reality is that during their tenure in the workforce, they have experienced a great amount of change, all of which have been implemented for regular use. For instance, this generation went from a world relying on phone calls and fax machines to the takeover of email and video conferencing. Baby Boomers can and will adapt to technology as long as the new tools are developed to make their work and lives easier (Marx, n.d.).

Baby Boomers are also in the unique position to both be a mentor and mentee within an organization. Since Boomers are less concerned right now with upward mobility, compared to Millennials, they are in an excellent position to serve as a mentor and help Gen X and Millennials within the organization. This helps make Baby Boomers feel appreciated and valued, which they like (Marx, n.d.). In some organizations, the practice of two-way mentoring is known as "transferring tribal knowledge" and has been used in organizations such as General Electric, Estee Lauder, and Saint-Gobain North America (Altany, 2019).

5.5 Organizational Culture and Generational Differences: Our Data

Perceptions about the strength of different dimensions of organizational culture were measured with the Organizational Culture Survey (Glaser, Zamanou, & Hacker, 1987). In addition to the overall scale, six sub-dimensions are included in the measure: Teamwork, Morale, Information Flow, Involvement, Supervision, and Meetings. Greater scores on this 5-point scale indicate greater endorsement of that sub-dimension of culture being present in their current organization. Overall, the average scores across all subscales were clustered above the midpoint, ranging from 3.33 to 3.66. Scores per generational group are presented in Table 5.1.

As the table demonstrates, there are differences by generation in only one of the six subscales and main scale: Morale. Gen X has a significantly lower morale score than both Baby Boomers and Millennials, who do not differ from one another. Gen X's dissatisfaction in the workplace has been demonstrated in other areas, as seen throughout other chapters in this volume. Similar outlooks on organizational culture represent an agreement in criteria for evaluating each of these facets of culture. The lack of differences in perceptions of culture is an interesting one.

The data from this study present interesting avenues for both practice within organizations and future research. What this demonstrates is that

Table 5.1 Generational Differences in the Organizational Culture Survey and Subscales

Measure	Baby Boomers M(SD)	Gen X M(SD)	Millennials M(SD)	F (2, 1147)	eta^2
Organizational Culture Survey	3.67(.77)	3.48(.85)	3.58(.78)	2.290	.00
Teamwork	3.69(.80)	3.55(.83)	3.60(.79)	1.046	.00
Morale	3.66(.90)[a]	**3.38(.1.03)**[b]	3.61(.94)[a]	5.747*	.01
Information Flow	3.56(.87)	3.44(.93)	3.52(.87)	.964	.00
Involvement	3.51(.99)	3.29(1.11)	3.39(.98)	1.653	.00
Supervision	3.75(.95)	3.62(.96)	3.67(.89)	.751	.00
Meetings	3.41(.91)	3.31(.95)	3.33(.94)	.385	.00

**p < .001, *p < .05.
[a,b]Significant differences between groups as determined by Tukey HSD post hocs. Scores that significantly differ from the other two scores are bolded.
Note: Morale differences between Gen X and Baby Boomers *p* = .051.

many organizations are already successfully retaining a multigenerational workforce, which is great news. This also demonstrates that while each generation has its own "wish list" of an ideal workplace, when various components of a workplace are simultaneously working in harmony, it creates an overall culture of satisfaction. For instance, meetings can help people feel involved, supervised, and part of a team.

It is important to note that this scale does not take generational desires into account, thereby making it more objective, but also less specific to generational differences that could still be present. It would be difficult for any organization to operate without any of the measures included here. That does not mean that these are the only measures related to culture. Further, this scale does not allow the inference that each generation is satisfied with the organizational culture.

5.6 Best Practices for Creating an Age-Inclusive Organizational Culture

Clarity and Communication

Clarifying the mission, values, and operations of the organization creates an organizational culture. Therefore, organizations should work hard to create clarity around these things then implement their communication about these concepts to existing employees as well as to future employees during recruitment. Working toward a shared goal can positively influence morale, teamwork, and involvement, all of which employees use to assess culture, as our data demonstrate. Moreover, knowing that generations take the values and mission of organizations seriously throughout their job searching process (see Chapter 4 for additional information), organizations should not let the opportunity to showcase their culture during recruitment pass by. Finally, communicating and showing how the organization actively works to fulfill its mission during the recruitment process helps with anticipatory socialization.

Assess Your Culture

Both organizational leaders and employees can assess the company culture that is present within the workplace. Doing this can help determine whether or not the actual culture is in alignment with the desired culture. Many of the steps for assessing organizational culture are similar to those outlined in Chapter 3 about internal communication. Beginning with a survey of all employees, including leaders, to understand how they perceive the culture is vital. This will encourage involvement for all employees, allowing them to share their thoughts, as well as provide information that is quantifiable, which can later be used to refine and refresh policies and operating procedures (Sanchez, 2011). An organizational culture measurement study can also be done using qualitative methods such as employee interviews or focus groups and/or observation. The results from a cultural study should then be examined against the desired culture and assessed with input from leadership so that there is a collective understanding of the current culture, ways to maintain it, and how to improve it in the future (Sanchez, 2011).

5.7 Conclusion

While the data from our study are consistent with that of other empirical research which does not show a major generational difference in perceptions of organizational culture, this is still an important finding. The information presented in this chapter coupled with our data shows that culture is holistic and communal. Organizational culture, when established well, can transcend age and experience levels to create an inclusive environment where everyone is happy, motivated, and encouraged to work toward the same goals guided by one central mission.

References

Ahmed, P. K. (1998). Culture and climate for innovation. *European Journal of Innovation Management, 1*, 30–43.

Allen, D. (2017). The merging of Gen X and Millennial cultures in the workplace. *ATD: Association for Talent Development.* Retrieved from https://www.td.org/insights/the-merging-of-gen-x-and-millennial-cultures-in-the-workplace

Altany, K. (2019). Baby Boomers vs. Millennials: Merging culture. Retrieved from https://www.industryweek.com/talent/article/22028374/baby-boomers-vs-millennials-merging-cultures

Alton, L. (2017). How millennials are reshaping what's important in corporate culture. *Forbes.* Retrieved from https://www.forbes.com/sites/larryalton/2017/06/20/how-millennials-are-reshaping-whats-important-in-corporate-culture/#f1da7222dfb8

Barney, J. (1986). Organizational culture: Can it be a source of sustained competitive advantage? *Academy of Management, 11*, 656–665.

Brack, J., & Kelly, K. (2012). Maximizing Millennials in the workplace. *UNC Kenan-Flagler Business School.* Retrieved from https://www.kenan-flagler.unc.edu/executive-development/custom-programs/~/media/files/documents/executive-development/maximizing-millennials-in-the-workplace.pdf

Braddy, P., Meade, A., & Kroustalis, C. (2006). Organizational recruitment website effects on viewers' perceptions of organizational culture. *Journal of Business and Psychology, 20*, 525–543.

Chew, J. (2016). Why Millennials would take a $7,600 pay cut for a new job. *Fortune.* Retrieved from http://fortune.com/2016/04/08/fidelity-millennial-study-career/

Corbin, L. (1977). Productivity and job satisfaction in research and development: Associated individual and supervisory variables. *Airforce Institute of Technology, 3.*

Deal, T., & Kennedy, A. (1982). *Corporate cultures.* Addison-Wesley.

DeLisi, P. S. (1990). Lessons from the steel axe: Culture, technology, and organizational change. *Sloan Management Review, 32*, 83–93.

Dubinsky, A., Howell, R., Ingram, T., & Bellenger, D. (1986). Salesforce socialization. *Journal of Marketing, 50*, 192–207.

Eisenberg, E., Trethewey, A., LeGreco, M., & Goodall, H. (2017). *Organizational communication: Balancing creativity and constraint* (8th ed.). Bedford St. Martin's.

Fayol, H. (1949). *General and industrial management.* Pitman.

Glaser, S. R., Zamanou, S., & Hacker, K. (1987). Measuring and interpreting organizational culture. *Management Communication Quarterly, 1*, 173–198.

Hofstede, G. (1994). *Uncommon sense about organizations: Case studies and field observations.* Sage.

Lorenzo, A. (1998). A framework for fundamental change: Context, criteria, and culture. *Community College, Journal of Research & Practice, 22*, 335–348.

Marx, L. (n.d.). How to create a company culture that Baby-Boomers, Millennials, and Gen Z employees can thrive in. Retrieved from: https://www.urbanbound.com/blog/how-to-create-a-company-culture-that-baby-boomers-millennials-and-gen-z-employees-can-thrive-in

Muchnick, M. (1996). *Naked management: Bare essentials for motivating the X-Generation at work.* St. Lucie Press.

Mulvanity, E. (2001). Generation X in the workplace: Age diversity issues in project teams. *Project Management Institute.* Retrieved from https://www.pmi.org/learning/library/generation-x-workplace-age-diversity-style-7904

Pettigrew, A. (1985). *The awakening giant: Continuity and change in imperial chemical industries.* Blackwell.

Pool, S. (2000). Organizational culture and its relationship between job tension in measuring outcomes among business executives. *Journal of Management Development, 19*, 32–49.

Porter, L., Lawler, E., & Hackman, J. (1975). *Behavior in organizations.* McGraw Hill.

Raines, C. (1997). *Beyond Generation X.* Crisp Publications.

Rashid, M., Sambasivan, M., & Rahman, A. (2004). The influence of organizational culture on attitudes toward organizational change. *Leadership & Organizational Development Journal, 25*, 161–179.

Rawlins, C., Indvik, J., & Johnson, P. (2008). Understanding the new generation: What the millennial cohort absolutely positively must have at work. *Journal of Organizational Culture, Communications and Conflict, 12*, 1–8.

Sanchez, P. (2011). Organizational culture. In T. Gillis (Ed.), *The IABC handbook of organizational communication* (pp. 28–40). Jossey-Bass.

Schein, E. (2010). *Organizational Culture and Leadership* (4th ed.). Josey-Bass.

Schneider, B., & Brief, A. (1996). Creating a climate and culture for sustainable organizational change. *Organizational Dynamics, 24*, 7–19.

Schneider, B., & Snyder, R. (1975). Some relationship between job satisfaction and organizational climate. *Journal of Applied Psychology, 60*, 318–328.

Sempane, M., Rieger, H., & Roodt, G. (2002). Job satisfaction in relation to organizational culture. *Journal of Industrial Psychology, 28*, 23–30.

Sheridan, J. (1992). Organizational culture and employee retention. *Academy of Management Journal, 35*, 1036–1056.

Silvester, J., & Anderson, N. (1999). Organizational culture change. *Journal of Occupational & Organizational Psychology, 72*, 1–24.

Smollan, R., & Sayers, J. (2009). Organizational culture, change and emotions: A qualitative study. *Journal of Change Management, 4*, 435–457.

Trompenaars, F., & Hampden-Turner, C. (1997). *Riding the waves of culture: Understanding diversity in global business.* McGraw Hill.

Umphress, E., Bingham, J., & Mitchell, M. (2010). Unethical behavior in the name of the company: The moderating effect of organizational identification and positive reciprocity beliefs on unethical pro-organizational behavior. *Journal of Applied Psychology, 95*, 769–780.

Wanous, J. (1977). Organization entry: Newcomers moving from outside to inside. *Psychological Bulletin, 84*, 601–618.

6 Organizational Identification

As part of the larger corporate structure, employees must still feel connected to the organization. This chapter will discuss how employees identify with and assimilate to the organization. We reflect on our own findings and connect these findings to previous literature surrounding organizational identification. Best practices will also be provided to help employees identify and connect to the organization as a whole.

6.1 Connecting to the Workplace

The traditional workplace involves people, processes, and plans. Because of this complexity, it is not enough to assume that people will feel connected to their organization simply by having a sense of belonging or accomplishment. Instead, several factors influence how and why employees feel like they are connected to their places of employment.

Employees tend to feel connected to their organizations when the socialization and assimilation processes have been effectively utilized. Employees, especially newly onboarded employees, must feel connected to their workgroups, other employees, and the larger organization as a whole (Morrison, 2002). Clear communication and relationship building can help build and sustain an employee's sense of belonging (Kammeyer-Mueller, Wanberg, Rubenstein, & Song, 2013).

Ultimately, the identity of the employee must be connected to the organization, and employees must be assimilated into the organization. As a result, retention and overall satisfaction may increase.

6.2 Identification

6.2.1 Previous Research and Theory

Identity manifests itself in many ways, especially in the organization. Identity, or "that which is central, distinctive, and more less enduring"

(Ashforth, 2016, p. 262), positions the identification concept as a personal distinctive that can be applied in organizations. Organizational identification includes one's linkage, or perceived link, to the organization. Cheney (1983), the original architect of the organizational identification questionnaire, believes identification is a process, specifically an active process whereby individuals link themselves to elements in that social scene. This link can lead to organizational commitment, i.e. retention (Cook and Wall, 1980). Thus, in the case of our study, an employee's central and distinct identity can be applied and developed within organizations, and, theoretically, the more an organization connects to an employee's central, distinct, and enduring identity, the more loyal an employee will remain.

Identification, while important especially as one enters an organization, is also an evolving concept. For one, scholars recognize that we continually re-negotiate our identity as it relates to an organization (Brown, 2017; Haslam, 2004). Further, as Kanungo (1982a) illustrates, job identification, rather than organizational commitment, can also include how committed one is to his or her professional position. In addition, identity to a position or an organization can manifest itself through concern with one's present position (Paullay, Alliger, & Stone-Romero, 1994), self-esteem related to job performance (Lodahl & Kejner, 1965), and genuine care and concern for one's work (Kanungo, 1982b). These elements, as one can imagine, tend to result in greater organizational effectiveness (Uygur & Kilic, 2009).

From a generational perspective, identification is felt differently depending on the general age group. And, ironically, for organizations to survive and thrive with a multigenerational workforce, organizations must deal not only with the social identity of their workers and the tendency to categorize ourselves and view other generations more positively or negatively depending on our perceptions (Ho & Yeung, 2020) but also with how this social identity connects to and infiltrates the workplace.

Generally, Baby Boomers, those affectionately referred to as career loyalists (Singh & Gupta, 2015), tend to find an identity in their jobs and are more likely to show a favorable attitude toward their job (Ng & Feldman, 2010). Historically, older workers view their jobs in a more positive light (Carstensen, 1991) and have received more gratification from the identification they find in their jobs (Wright & Hamilton, 1978). Generation X, those who tend to be more independent and self-reliant, are viewed as less loyal than their Boomer coworkers and Boomer bosses (Rottier, 2001) although a study by Davis, Pawlowski, & Houston (2016) reveals that Boomers and Generation X tend to be more alike in their work and job involvement as well as organizational and professional commitment. Compared to Baby Boomers and Gen-Xers, Millennials tend to be more concerned, overall, with their identity and organizational identifications. Millennials are usually more attracted to and identify more uniquely with organizations and institutions where there the system is equitable. To put it another way, despite public opinion that would decry millennials as disloyal, millennials tend to be loyal to those organizations which are loyal to them (Hershatter & Epstein, 2010). All of this impacts how one's identity is connected to and developed within the organization, and because of generational differences related to organizational identification, job identification, workplaces—regardless of the industry—would do well to establish clearer opportunities for their workers to connect to the organization at large. As workers strive to identify with their organizations, the topic needs continual study, and it is important to consider the extent to which individuals identify with the organization. And, while worker identification is an important generational consideration, how workers assimilate in their organizations and how organizations retain their employees are also important to note for those interested in organizational dynamics.

6.2.2 Organizational Identification and Generational Difference: Our Data

Cheney's (1983) Organizational Identification Scale offers a unidimensional approach to assessing the degree to which individuals identify with their organization. Across all three generations, this scale reported excellent reliability (Cronbach's alpha = .943) and mean just above its midpoint (M = 3.76 (SD = 1.24) on a 7-point scale.

A look at differences in means across the generational groups show small, yet marginally significant differences between groups. An ANOVA showed overall small, significant differences, $F(2, 1148) = 3.356$, partial eta^2 = .006, $p < .05$ across the three groups. Millennials reported the greatest identification with their organization (M = 4.31, SD = 1.20), followed by Baby Boomers (M = 4.11, SD = 1.31) and Gen X (M = 4.10, SD = 1.31). A Tukey post hoc test revealed the difference between Gen X and Millennials neared significance (p = .053).

The data from our study show that individuals' identification with their organization does not differ to a large degree by their generation. However, we see a small, and nearly significant difference: Millennials have the greatest identification with their organization as measured here. This is in line with previous research.

6.3 Assimilation

6.3.1 Previous Research and Theory

Through organizational assimilation, employees learn about the organization as a whole and learn about the organization's members, policies, procedures, culture, and other crucial aspects of the workplace that employees need to grasp (Croucher, Zeng, & Kassing, 2016). In 2003, Myers and Oetzel developed six dimensions of the organizational assimilation process. Their dimensions include *familiarity* with others, specifically the ability to develop and build relationships; *acculturation*, or the process of learning about organizational norms; *recognition*, being recognized as a valuable member of the organization by the organization; *involvement*, ways to contribute to the organization; *job competency*, or one's actual job performance; and *role negotiation*, or the process an employee goes through to negotiate their actual place or expectations within an organization. The sections that follow explore these dimensions from a generational perspective.

Familiarity

As employees assimilate into the organization, they can develop a familiarity with those other coworkers, especially supervisors. Ironically, Millennials and Gen Xers share similar perspectives on work, and their understanding tends to run counter to a Boomer perspective. Generally, for Millennials and X-ers alike, their identity is not as focused on their job (Marston, 2007). This can become a point of contention between generations in organizations and can, therefore, negatively impact how relationships are developed (Raines, 2003). As these relationships form—especially now as Boomers are still primarily supervisors—generally, in organizational contexts, these relationships become even more delicate, and familiarity becomes even more important. As Jokisaari and Nurmi (2009) found, strong relationships with supervisors help develop long-term job satisfaction for millennials. This means organizations should enhance opportunities for cross-generational relationship building. However, this may be easier than it sounds because several factors influence how we come to build and sustain relationships at work.

Obviously, trust can influence how individuals develop and build relationships, especially with supervisors. As members of different organizations strive to build effective relationships, age diversity can continually get in the way as intergenerational differences can influence the trust one has for members of their team or their supervisors/subordinates (Williams, 2016). It is important, then, to step back and recognize that in order for generational assimilation to occur successfully, there must be a foundation of trust. In organizations where communication is a prominent mechanism for culture, understanding, and general functionality, clear expectations for workplace relationships are necessary. For one, Millennials tend to expect closer relationships and greater transparency from their supervisors (Society for Human Resource Management, 2009). And it is likely that Generation Z supervisor expectations will follow a similar, or even more intense, trajectory (Goh & Lee, 2018). Familiarity and relationship building, then, become a crucial factor for assimilating workers, especially younger employees, into the organization.

Acculturation

Familiarity with members of the organization should be preceded by an acculturation process whereby the employee is immersed in an understanding of organizational norms and culture. Myers and Oetzel (2003) also focus not just on learning behavioral norms but on avoiding those actions that may go against or break organizational norms. While organizational norms look differently depending on the organization, one generational impact on organizational acculturation was the relationship between supervisor and employee. In most cases, for instance, Baby Boomers were probably taught to accept direction, criticism, feedback, etc. from a supervisor and to subsequently not question the comments (Stewart, Oliver, Cravens, & Oishi, 2017). For Millennials, generally, this organizational norm is archaic. Interestingly, Stewart et al. (2017) also argue that millennials, compared to previous generations, carry an expectation that the workplace will cater to or accommodate their needs. This understanding, coupled with the notion that organizational norms may be of less importance to millennials, means organizations should consider how to approach acculturation as a valuable standard rather than a burdensome reality.

Recognition

Generally, all employees want and need recognition in the workplace. While the type and amount of recognition may be preferential, generations across the spectrum want to know that they have performed at or above expectations (Van Dyke & Ryan, 2013). Recognition, the understanding that an employee is of value to their organization, can manifest itself in increased wages or even through additional perks like flexible hours or remote work (Meister & Willyerd, 2010). Ironically, rewards like remuneration and benefits and a positive working environment are more important to the younger employees and tend to reduce as employees get older (Close & Martins, 2015). Twenge and Campbell (2010) also argue that Millennials, compared to Baby Boomers, are more interested in extrinsic rewards but less interested compared to Generation X employees. Millennials also prefer non-traditional or non-material rewards more than their generational counterparts do and greatly appreciate learning and development and immediate feedback from supervisors (Hewlett, Sherbin, & Sumberg, 2009). These generational differences force managers to recognize the employees as individuals, understanding that a one-size-fits all reward system is outdated.

Involvement

Employee involvement in the organization, or the actual ways one contributes to the workplace, can manifest itself in a variety of ways. Boomers, for instance, can be seen by some as problematic not because of their contributions but rather because of their inability or unwillingness to adapt to a changing workplace (Bosco & Harvey, 2013). In terms of asset accumulation, Boomers are retiring with more wealth than any previous generation; while this is not a direct indicator of workplace productivity, it can shed some light on Boomer organizational and economic impact (Roberts, 2011). In a 2005 study, specifically looking at the differences in productivity between Boomers and Gen Xers, Appelbaum, Serena, & Shapiro found that older workers are more productive than younger workers due to their experience and knowledge. Long held notions that younger employees who are first starting out tend to produce more immediate results may not be entirely true. Instead, it is important to recognize that employee involvement and contributions may be linked as much to experience as anything else. However, Martin (2005) indicates that Generation Y, otherwise known as Millennials, if led by the right type of manager, have the potential to be the highest performing generation in history. This holistic understanding, that Generation Y has immense productivity potential, serves researchers well as they consider the multigenerational workplace. There are no substitutes for experience, but because of their technology acumen, entrepreneurial spirit, and achievement personality, Millennials may become dominant producers in organizational contexts.

Job Competency

In a similar vein to involvement, job competency involves one's actual job performance. While not a generational difference per se, it is important to note that historically researchers would agree that there is little to no relationship between age and job performance (Salthouse & Maurer, 1996; Warr, 1994). Job performance or competency, like involvement, can be influenced by experience and accumulated job knowledge, thus making someone who has been in a position longer potentially more efficient. Further, job performance may also filter down to different generations in the workplace as younger generations may see increased productivity because of the transferable experience of older generations through mentorship or collaborative projects (Waljee, Vineet, & Saint, 2020). As workers navigate their actual performance on the job, generational differences can be useful for considering improved productivity related to collaboration and individual duties.

Role Negotiation

The final dimension for Myers and Oetzel (2003), role negotiation, explores the process an employee goes through to negotiate their actual place or expectations within an organization. Practically speaking, role negotiation is how one perceives he or she fits within an organization. While other generations are not immune to the challenges associated with role negotiation in organizations, Millennials, because of stereotypes about them as well as their own expectations, may struggle with organizational socialization (Marston, 2007). Internal role negotiation is also determined by membership negotiation, where current organizational members decide who may, or may not, suffice as an appropriate organizational fit (Slaughter & Zickar, 2006). Those just entering positions also participate in this negotiation process (Scott & Myers, 2010). Ironically, Millennial roles will be influenced by their own perceptions, and these expectations may also impact the role(s) of others within the organization (Myers & Sadaghiani, 2010). How these negotiated roles within an organization, especially with the incoming Generation Z cohort filtering in slowly, affect long-term organizational culture is yet to be determined.

6.3.1 Organizational Assimilation and Generational Difference: Our Data

Meyers and Oetzel's (2003) Organizational Assimilation Index demonstrated excellent reliability (Cronbach's alpha = .938) and a mean score

Table 6.1 Generational Differences in the Organizational Assimilation Index and Subscales

Measure	Baby Boomers M(SD)	Gen X M(SD)	Millennials M(SD)	F (2, 1147)	eta^2
Organizational Assimilation Index	4.03(.68)[a]	3.82(.80)[a]	**3.76(.73)[b]**	5.77*	.01
Supervisor Familiarity	3.83(.90)	3.72(1.03)	3.75(.97)	.425	.00
Acculturation	4.47(.72)[a]	4.24(.89)[a]	**4.13(.83)[b]**	7.80**	.01
Recognition	**4.17(.92)[b]**	3.83(1.14)[a]	3.83(.99)[a]	4.860*	.01
Involvement	3.57(1.04)	3.37(1.12)	3.41(1.05)	1.20	.00
Job Competency	4.18(.72)[a]	4.03(.80)[a]	**3.82(.80)[b]**	13.574**	.02
Role Negotiation	**3.97(.92)[a]**	3.84(1.00)[b]	3.64((1.00)[b]	7.325**	.01

*$p < .001$, **$p < .05$.
[a,b]Significant differences between groups as determined by Tukey HSD post hocs. Scores which significantly differ from the other two scores are bolded.

well above the midpoint across all individuals ($M = 380$, $SD = .74$). Greater scores are indicative of greater assimilation and its sub-dimensions. Results are presented below in Table 6.1. Millennials scored significantly lower ($M = 3.76$, $SD = .73$) than both Gen X ($M = 3.82$, $SD = .80$) and Baby Boomers ($M = 4.03$, $SD = .68$), who did not significantly differ, despite the differences in mean scores.

The pattern of Millennials scoring significantly lower is a pattern found in the subdimensions of the scale as well. In two of the sub-scales, Millennials scored significantly lower than both Gen X and Baby Boomers (acculturation, job competency); in another two subscales, both Millennials and Gen X scored significantly lower than Baby Boomers (recognition, role negotiation), and there were no differences in the remaining two subscales (supervisor familiarity, involvement). While these differences are small in effect size, the pattern observed is relatively consistent: Millennials demonstrate lower scores across the subdimensions of assimilation, Baby Boomers demonstrate greater scores, and Gen X falls in between. It should be noted that across all participants, scores on organizational identification and organizational assimilation share a $r = .306$, $p < .01$. This moderate-size correlation speaks to the relatedness of the two concepts.

6.4 Retention

Optimizing talent, specifically hiring and retaining, is a significant challenge facing modern organizations (Clare, 2009). The elements listed above related to assimilation must be negotiated in an effective manner for employees to stay at organizations. At times, leaving a company cannot be helped. However, there are certainly instances when workers will leave an organization because they found a better opportunity, have not assimilated themselves into the broader culture, or believe they are not being used effectively in their current role. Baby Boomers still have a desire to work and participate actively in organizations (Salb, 2015). Because many Boomers are career loyalists, retention was not a necessary focus. Retention, partly because Generation X-ers were more inclined to leave their positions for something else, was more important with those who came after Boomers. Those employing Generation X need to offer variety, simulation, and constant change to keep workers engaged (Jurkiewicz, 2000). Jurkiewicz (2000) also notes that culture is of primary importance for X-ers. This trend has continued, and today employee retention is a renewed area of study.

Generational workplace preferences do vary, although some of the foundational desires of employees transcend generational demographics. For one, Eversole, Venneberg, and Crowder (2012) emphasize the importance of organizational flexibility to retain workers across the generational spectrum. Pregnolato, Bussin, and Schlecter (2017), when evaluating reward preferences of different generations, reveal that financial rewards, including benefits; performance and recognition; remuneration; and career; as well as career advancement; learning; and work-life balance are all elements that can help organizations retain talented employees. Generation Z, those post-millennial workers, likewise appreciate a career path, flexible work conditions, and transparency (Goh & Okumus, 2020). Despite their simplicity, these components are difficult to achieve in organizations.

6.5 Best Practices for Helping Employees Identify with the Organization

The integration of multiple generations into the workplace can create organizational uncertainty. Organizations should strive to create environments where employees feel as though they belong and know they are valuable members. The following best practices can help employees identify with their organization, thus contributing to assimilation and retention mechanisms that transcend generational boundaries.

Best Practice 1: Build a Mission-Centric Culture

Employees, generally, respond more positively to organizations where they feel connected. This is especially true for members of Generation Z as well as Millennials. Yet, Gen X-ers and Baby Boomers also want to know that their work has value. Organizations would do well to create a mission-centric culture that is inclusive of all backgrounds and perspectives. But, ultimately, reminding employees of the mission and articulating how each individual employee "fits" into the broader work can be helpful.

Best Practice 2: Communicate Clearly

A sense of belonging does not occur naturally and, instead, must be communicated from the supervisory level and through peer relationships. Communicate expectations and explore ways to deliver messages in ways that resonate with individual employees, not just the group as a whole. As you onboard employees, you must also communicate effectively as the assimilation process starts.

Best Practice 3: Start Building Relationships Early and Often

Employees must be familiar with the organization and their role within the broader structure. This familiarity occurs over time, but you can develop mentorship relationships, especially across the generational spectrum, that help younger workers integrate, encourage older workers to leave a legacy of impact, and establish a culture of relationship development throughout the organization.

6.6 Conclusion

Our data show an interesting connection to previous research. Millennials want and need to feel connected to the institution. Assimilation, and the subsequent connection that follows, is key to establishing rapport with younger employees and can help retain and even recruit Millennial talent. It is important to continue to stress to all employees, especially younger generations, that training for the job will be provided and that the culture, as a whole, is employee friendly and generally positive.

References

Appelbaum, S. H., Serena, M., & Shapiro, B. T. (2005). Generation "X" and the Boomers: An analysis of realities and myths. *Management Research News, 28*, 1–33. https://doi.org/10.1108/01409170510784751

Ashforth, B. E. (2016). Exploring identity and identification in organizations: Time for some course correction. *Journal of Leadership and Organizational Studies, 23*, 361–373. doi: 10.1177/1548051816667897

Bosco, S. M., & Harvey, D. M. (2013). Generational effects on recruitment and workplace productivity. *Northeast Business and Economics Association Proceedings*, 17–20.

Brown, A. D. (2017). Identity work and organizational identification. *International Journal of Management Reviews, 19*, 296–317. doi: 10.1111/ijmr.12152

Carstensen, L. L. (1991). Selectivity theory: Social activity in life-span context. In K. W. Sehaie (Ed.), *Annual review of gerontology and geriatrics* (pp. 195–217). Springer.

Cheney, G. (1983). On the various and changing meanings of organizational membership: Field study of organizational identification. *Communication Monographs, 50*, 342–362.

Clare, C. (2009). Generational differences: Turning challenges into opportunities. *Journal of Property Management, 74*, 40–41.

Close, D., & Martins, N. (2015). Generational motivation and preference for reward and recognition. *Journal of Governance and Regulation, 4*, 259–270.

Cook, J., & Wall, T. (1980). New work attitude measures of trust, organizational commitment and personal need non-fulfillment. *Journal of Occupational Psychology, 53*, 39–52.

Croucher, S. M., Zeng, C., & Kassing, J. (2016). Learning to contradict and standing up for the company: An exploration of the relationship between organizational dissent, organizational assimilation, and organizational reputation. *International Journal of Business Communication, 56*, 349–367. https://doi.org/10.1177%2F2329488416633852

Davis, J. B., Pawlowski, S. D., & Houston, A. (2016). Work commitments of Baby Boomers and Gen-Xers in the IT profession: Generational differences or myth? *Journal of Computer Information Systems, 46*, 43–49. https://doi.org/10.1080/08874417.2006.11645897

Eversole, B. A. W., Venneberg, D. L., & Crowder, C. L. (2012). Creating a flexible organizational culture to attract and retain talented workers across generations. *Advances in Developing Human Resources, 14*, 607–625. https://doi.org/10.1177%2F1523422312455612

Goh, E., & Lee, C. (2018). A workforce to be reckoned with: The emerging pivotal Generation Z hospitality workforce. *International Journal of Hospitality Management, 73*, 20–28. https://doi.org/10.1016/j.ijhm.2018.01.016

Goh, E., & Okumus, F. (2020). Avoiding the hospitality workforce bubble: Strategies to attract and retain Generation Z talent in the hospitality workforce. *Tourism Management Perspectives, 33*, 1–7. https://doi.org/10. 1016/j.tmp.2019.100603

Haslam, S. A. (2004). *Psychology in organizations: The social identity approach* (2nd ed.). Sage.

Hershatter, A., & Epstein, M. (2010). Millennials and the world of work: An organization and management perspective. *Journal of Business Psychology, 25*, 211–223. doi:10.1007/s10869-010-9160-y

Hewlett, S. A., Sherbin, L., & Sumberg, K. (2009). How Gen Y & boomers will reshape your agenda. *Harvard Business Review, 87*, 71–76.

Ho, H. C. Y., & Yeung, D. Y. (2020). Conflict between younger and older workers: An identity-based approach. *International Journal of Conflict Management*, 1–24. doi:http://dx.doi.org/10.1108/IJCMA-08-2019-0124

Jokisaari, M., & Nurmi, J. E. (2009). Change in newcomers' supervisor support and socialization outcomes after organizational entry. *Academy of Management Journal, 52*, 527–544.

Jurkiewicz, C. L. (2000). Generation X and the public employee. *Public Personnel Management, 29*, 55–74. https://doi.org/10.1177%2F009102600002900105

Kammeyer-Mueller, J. D., Wanberg, C. R., Rubenstein, A., & Song, Z. (2013). Support, undermining, and newcomer socialization: Fitting in during the first 90 days. *Academy of Management Journal, 56*, 1104–1124. https://doi.org/10. 5465/amj.2010.0791

Kanungo, R. N. (1982a). Measurement of job and work involvement. *Journal of Applied Psychology, 67*, 341–349.

Kanungo, R. (1982b). *Work alienation: An integrative approach*. Wiley.

Lodahl, T. M., & Kejner, M. (1965). The definition and measurement of job involvement. *Journal of Applied Psychology, 49*, 24–33.

Marston, C. (2007). *Motivating the what's in it for me workforce: Managing across the generational divide and increase profits*. John Wiley & Sons, Inc.

Martin, C. A. (2005). From high maintenance to high productivity: What managers need to know about Generation Y. *Industrial and Commercial Training, 1*, 39–44. https://doi.org/10.1108/00197850510699965

Meister, J. and Willyerd, K. (2010). *The 2020 workplace*. HarperCollins.

Morrison, E. W. (2002). Newcomers' relationships: The role of social network ties during socialization. *Academy of Management Journal, 45*, 1149–1160. https://doi.org/10.5465/3069430

Myers, K. K., & Oetzel, J. G. (2003). Exploring the dimensions of organizational assimilation: Creating and validating a measure. *Communication Quarterly, 51*, 438–457. https://doi.org/10.1080/01463370309370166

Myers, K. K., & Sadaghiani, K. (2010). Millennials in the workplace: A communication perspective on Millennials' organizational relationships and performance. *Journal of Business and Psychology, 25*, 225–238.

Ng, T. W. H., & Feldman, D. C. (2010), The relationships of age with job attitudes: A meta-analysis. *Personnel Psychology, 63*(3), 677–718.

Paullay, I., Alliger, G., & Stone-Romero, E. (1994). Construct validation of two instruments designed to measure job involvement and work centrality. *Journal of Applied Psychology, 79*, 224–228.

Pregnolato, M., Bussin, M. H. R., & Schlecter, A. F. (2017). Total rewards that retain: A study of demographic preferences. *SA Journal of Human Resource Management, 15*, 1–10. doi: 10.4102/sajhrm.v15.804

Raines, C. (2003). *Connecting generations: The sourcebook for a new workplace.* Thompson Crisp Learning.

Roberts, K. (2011). The end of the long baby-boomer generation. *Journal of Youth Studies, 4*, 479–497. https://doi.org/10.1080/13676261.2012.663900

Rottier, A. (2001). Gen 2001: loyalty and values, *Workforce, 80*, 23.

Salb, D. (2015). Using technology to retain Baby Boomers in the workplace. *Computer and Information Science, 8*, 180–185. doi:10.5539/cis.v8n3p180

Salthouse, T. A., & Maurer, T. J. (1996). Aging, job performance, and career development. In J. E. Birren, K. W. Schaie, R. P. Abeles, M. Gatz, & T. A. Salthouse (Eds.), *Handbook of the psychology of aging* (4th ed., pp. 353–365). Academic Press.

Scott, C. W., & Myers, K. K. (2010). Toward an integrative theoretical perspective of membership negotiations: Socialization, assimilation, and the duality of structure. *Communication Theory, 30*, 79–105.

Singh, A., & Gupta, B. (2015). Job involvement, organizational commitment, professional commitment, and team commitment: A study of generational diversity. *Benchmarking: An International Journal, 22*, 1192–1211.

Slaughter, J. E., & Zickar, M. J. (2006). A new look at the role of insiders in the newcomer socialization process. *Group & Organization Management, 31*, 264–290.

Society for Human Resource Management. (2009). *The multigenerational workforce: Opportunity for competitive success.* http://www.shrm.org/Research/Articles/Articles/Documents/09-0027_RQ_March_2009_FINAL_noad.pdf

Stewart, J. S., Oliver, E. G., Cravens, K. S., & Oishi, S. (2017). Managing millennials: Embracing generational differences. *Business Horizons, 60*, 45–54. https://doi.org/10.1016/j.bushor.2016.08.011

Twenge, J., & Campbell, S. (2010). Who are the Millennials? Empirical evidence for generational differences in work values, attitudes and personality. In E. Ng, S. Lyons, & L. Schweitzer (Eds.), *Managing the new workforce* (pp. 1–19). Edward Elgar Publishing.

Uygur, A., & Kilic, G. (2009). A study into organizational commitment and job involvement: An application towards the personnel in the central organization for ministry of health in Turkey. *Ozean Journal of Applied Sciences, 2*, 113–125.

Van Dyke, M., & Ryan, M. (2013). Changing the compensation conversation and the growing utility of non-cash rewards and recognition. *Compensation and Benefits Review,44*, 276–279.

Williams, M. (2016). Being trusted: How team generational age diversity promotes and undermines trust in cross-boundary relationships. *Journal of Organizational Behavior, 37,* 346–373.

Warr, P. (1994). Age and employment. In M. Dunnette, L. Hough, & H. Triandis (Eds.), *Handbook of industrial and organizational psychology* (pp. 487–550). Consulting Psychologists Press.

Waljee, J. F., Vineet, C., & Saint, S. (2020). Mentoring millennials. *JAMA, 17,* 1716–1717. doi:10.1001/jama.2020.3085

Wright, J. D., & Hamilton, R. F. (1978). Work satisfaction and age: Some evidence for the 'job change' hypothesis. *Social Forces, 56,* 1140–1158.

7 Communication in the Organization: Positive Communication

This chapter will explore, specifically, supportive workplace communication by focusing on mentorship and communication support. The authors will reflect on their findings and connect these findings to previous literature surrounding mentorship and supportive communication.

7.1 Supportive Communication

The workplace is unique because it is a place where different contexts of communication converge. We have to manage interpersonal relationships and stakeholder communication as well as maintain our professional self-image simultaneously. While people are familiar with the various conflicts and dilemmas that can occur due to communication – or rather miscommunications – in the workplace, there is also a vast body of research that explores the ways in which communication helps engage employees and keep them happy, supported, and satisfied in the workplace.

Public relations helps to understand communication within the organization and between organizations and an external audience (customers, community leaders, etc.). Excellence theory is one of the most foundational theories to inform public relations and gives way to understanding supportive communication. The essence of excellence theory is that the most effective communication is two-way and symmetrical (Grunig & Grunig, 2008). This means that both parties engaged in communication are speaking and listening equally. Operating with this theory in mind helps inform supportive communication in the workplace while also helping with employee trust and engagement efforts.

Supportive communication is defined as "verbal and nonverbal behavior produced with the intention of providing assistance to others perceived as needing that aid" (Burleson & MacGeorge, 2002, p. 374). Previous research helps to understand the various benefits of supportive communication, an area that has been robustly studied in health and interpersonal contexts, especially. For instance, supportive communication has been demonstrated to create and strengthen social networks, improve social experiences, and provide greater perceptions of available support (Burleson, 2009; Cohen, Mermelstein, Karmarck, & Hoberman, 1985; Shaver, 2008). Furthermore, supportive communication can decrease emotional distress and help people cope more easily (Cunningham & Barbee, 2000; Gottlieb, 1994). Research about supportive communication has also demonstrated that supportive messages are complex and that the effectiveness of messages is contingent upon various factors, including the message source, the receiver of the message, and the interactional context (Bodie & Burleson, 2008; Cutrona, Cohen, & Igram, 1990).

Burleson (2009) outlines features of supportive messages, which apply to both professional and interpersonal interactions. The first feature is the message content, which includes verbal and nonverbal communication. The verbal content is what the person seeking the support actually says to solicit the need for support from someone else and the type of support offered through the verbal message. Different types of support include emotional support, informational support or advice, esteem support, and/or social network support. The nonverbal elements of a message can include the length of the message, the timing or placement of the message within an interaction, how the message is shared, and the number of appeals or statements in the message (Feng, 2009; Jacobson, 1986; Neff & Karney, 2005).

The second feature of supportive communication is the relationship that exists between the person needing support and the person providing the support. Women tend to be viewed as more supportive than men, and messages provided by women are evaluated as more supportive than those typically provided by men, even when the content of the message is the same (Glynn, Christenfeld, & Gerin, 1999; Uno, Uchino, & Smith, 2002). The credibility of the helper is also known to influence supportive communication messages, as well as the quality of the relationship between the two parties. When the person receiving support feels close to the one providing support, messages are evaluated more favorably (Clark et al., 1998).

The final two features include the context and the recipient. Features of the context refer to the physical setting, the medium of communication, and the problem situation that makes supportive communication a relevant activity (Burleson, 2009). For instance, unsolicited messages are viewed unfavorably, and the quality of support is more impactful when it is related to a serious issue (Burleson, 2009; MacGeorge, Feng, & Thompson, 2008). Finally, features of the recipient matter, making this timely for consideration within a multigenerational workforce. Demographic characteristics, personality composition, and cognitive attributes influence responses to supportive communication (Burleson, 2009).

7.2 Supportive Communication in the Workplace

The workplace creates endless opportunities for uncertainty, which creates the need for support. The workplace can also be a stressful environment, which furthers our need and desire for support. This is why people so often turn to their coworkers for post-work happy hours, sessions where everyone can vent their frustrations, and interoffice relationships, all of which can be considered support, albeit not always healthy support. Supportive communication in the workplace seeks to help manage and reduce uncertainty (Mikkola, 2019). The benefits of supportive communication at work are plentiful, including increases in productivity, motivation, job satisfaction, and commitment. Supportive workplace relationships can also help with problemsolving, decision making, and learning.

Mikkola (2019) outlines two types of support present in the workplace: emotional and informational support. Emotional support is what enables employees to become friends, share frustrations, and celebrate each other's accomplishments. Emotional support is used to help gain psychological distance from the emotions that can erupt during stressful and uncertain workplace situations. Through emotional support, employees help each other lessen the amount of emotional distress one or both of them may be experiencing (Burleson, 2003). A central feature of emotional support is legitimizing the feelings of the person seeking support through verbal and nonverbal communication. Informational support, on the other hand, provides relevant information to reduce uncertainty as a form of support (Brashers, 2001). Informational support is best suited to situations that are problem and solution oriented, whereas many emotional support situations cannot be solved through information.

Supportive communication and social support provide various positive outcomes in the workplace, as evidenced by previous research. For example, social support promotes high-quality performance through increasing emotional affirmation and strengthening the capacity for collective problem-solving (Park, Wilson, & Lee, 2004). Social support can also boost engagement among both employees and leaders alike, which is an antecedent to organizational commitment (Lambert, Minor, Wells, & Hogan, 2016). Similarly, when people work in a supportive environment, it can prevent and decrease employee turnover (Feeley, Moon, Kozey, & Lowe, 2010). Social support in the workplace helps reduce stress among employees, which positively influences levels of job satisfaction and helps prevent burnout (Singh, Singh, & Singhi, 2015; Snyder, 2009).

7.3 Mentorship

Mentoring is an oft-studied organizational concept that is practiced in prevalence across industries. In fact, mentoring has become somewhat of a buzzword in both empirical and mass media contexts and has been studied both extensively and empirically in U.S. workplaces. While often viewed as a way to promote advancement among disadvantaged groups such as women and/or BIPOC and minorities who lack access to informal and interpersonal career development resources, mentoring programs have been implemented at organizations throughout the United States.

A clear definition of mentoring is a controversial subject, but in essence, mentoring relationships consist between one seasoned or more senior member of an organization and one more junior member of the organization. Mentoring is unique because it can create an unequal and vulnerable relationship. A mentor is also defined as a person who serves as a guide or sponsor to the development of another who has a different rank (Sands, Parson, & Duane, 1991). The most traditional, common, and concise definition of workplace mentoring is a relationship between two people (dyadic) where the senior employee takes the junior employee under his or her wing to share knowledge and provide guidance (Allen, Finkelstein, & Poteet, 2009).

Mentoring has roots in Greek mythology and later evolved into the modern day understanding of a protege, similar to apprenticeship. Mentoring used to be most prevalent among men, where midlife men served as transitional figures for younger men during their early adulthood (Levinson, Darrow, Klein, Levinson, & McKeen, 1978). Mentoring has since evolved into a mentor/mentee relationship and away from the protege conceptualization and practice. Mentees are guided and advised by mentors, who are senior-level role models who provide career guidance, coaching, and support through an ongoing relationship (Darling, 1985; Prehm and Iscson, 1985). Mentees should take an active role in the formation and development of mentoring relationships. Good mentors should be "sincere in their dealings with mentees, be able to listen actively and understand mentees' needs, and have a well-established position within the [organization]." (Sambunjak, Straus, & Marusic, p. 79, 2009).

Mentoring is inherently supportive and provides two forms of support: career-related and psychosocial support. Career-related support focuses on the success, development, and advancement of the mentee. This can include helping the mentee gain exposure and visibility; coaching; providing protection and sponsorship; and providing opportunities for assignments. Psychosocial support, on the other hand, focuses more on the identity of the mentee and building his or her effectiveness as a professional. This includes activities such as helping them make friends, building acceptance and confirmation, and serving as a role model. The psychosocial elements of mentoring have been shown to be positively associated with the outcomes of the mentoring relationship (Allen et al., 2009).

Mentoring is fundamentally different from other types of workplace relationships. First, mentoring is a dyadic relationship between people of two different experience levels. Second, it is both a mutually beneficial relationship but also asymmetrical because the focus of the relationship is on the development of the mentee, despite the benefits that both parties can gain. Finally, mentoring is a fluid and dynamic relationship that changes over time. It differs from supervisor–subordinate relationships, for instance, because the mentor and the mentee are not required to work together, there is no requirement for reward power to be present, and the mentor can be several levels higher than the mentee – or only one level higher (Allen et al., 2009).

Jacobi (1991) explicated five elements that are present in the mentoring relationship: 1) focus on achievement or acquisition of knowledge; 2) emotional and psychological support, direct assistance with career and professional development, and role modeling; 3) reciprocity where both mentor and mentee derive benefits; 4) personal in nature involving direct interaction; and 5) emphasizes the mentor's greater experience, influence, and achievement within a particular organization. This demonstrates the complexity of mentoring and reinforces the notion that leaders are essential to the process of developing supportive and collaborative cultures (Edge, 2014).

Mentoring offers benefits for the mentor, the mentee, and the organization, making it well suited for a multigenerational workforce where people with various levels of experience and knowledge are working together. Mentors, for example, experience enhanced career success, which is great for members for Gen X, career revitalization which can be important for Baby Boomers, and personal growth and satisfaction. Conversely, mentees experience higher compensation and faster salary growth, more promotions and higher expectations for advancement, more job and career satisfaction, and greater commitment to the organization. All of these benefits are very important to Millennial employees, making them well positioned to receive mentoring from a Gen X or Boomer employee. Finally, organizations can experience benefits such as enhanced recruitment and retention efforts and increases in employee socialization and organizational learning (Allen et al., 2009).

As the multigenerational workforce became the norm and organizations had three, sometimes four generations present, a new type of mentoring emerged: reverse mentoring. Reverse mentoring flips traditional mentoring upside down and has a younger, junior employee serving as the mentor to an older, senior colleague (Murphy, 2012). The concept was first introduced by Jack Welsh, CEO of General Electric, but is now considered a best practice at other large organizations including Dell, Estee Lauder, Procter & Gamble, and Time Warner (Greengard, 2002; Harvey & Buckley, 2002; Hewlett, Sherbin, & Sumberg, 2009). One of the main benefits of reverse mentoring is the ability for others to learn from the digital wisdom and savviness of younger generations. Additionally, though, reverse mentoring helps prepare younger employees for leadership roles, fosters diversity efforts, enhances and promotes intergenerational working relationships, and promotes innovation (Murphy, 2012). Furthermore, reverse mentoring, much like traditional mentoring, is a cost-effective professional development strategy for organizations to implement.

7.4 Previous Research and Theory

Mentoring and communication support are frequently studied together because they are antecedents to so many other workplace variables as mentioned throughout this chapter. The mentoring and communication support scale, used in our study, is one of the most commonly applied scales for measurement empirically. The scale was originally developed to study communication within academic organizations but has since been applied to the nonacademic workforce. The scale is useful because it recognizes that mentoring is part of the larger concept of workplace support, while also maintaining the unique attributes of mentoring. The mentoring and communication support scale helps to determine mentoring as well as other supportive behaviors dimensionally (Hill, Bahniuk, Dobos, & Rouner, 1989).

Empirical research utilizing the mentoring and communication support scale has helped researchers to better understand the positive attributes of a supportive workplace that includes mentoring. For instance, Harris, Winskowski, and Engdahl (2007) demonstrated that social support accounted for almost 17% of the variance in job satisfaction, with career mentoring being one of the most predictive factors of job satisfaction. A case study using two large chemical organizations demonstrated that mentoring as part of a larger organizational communication support program helps minority employees climb the corporate ladder, as well as gain friendships, feel supported, and maintain a positive attitude in the workplace (Kogler Hill & Gant, 2000). A management study examined the mutuality present in mentoring and supportive communication finding that when mentees are open to coaching and put forth effort in accomplishing work, mentors' perceptions of relationship effectiveness and trust are positively influenced. Furthermore, when mentors engage in supportive behaviors to meet the expectations of mentees, mentees form higher perceptions of effectiveness and trust for their mentor (Young & Perrewe, 2000). Collectively, this research helps showcase the positive outcomes and importance of mentoring and supportive communication in the workplace, which is further demonstrated through our data in what follows.

7.5 Mentoring and Communication Support and Generational Differences: Our Data

The Mentoring and Communication Support Scale (Hill et al., 1989) indexed participants' experiences of mentoring and communication support in their workplaces. This scale contains four subscales: Career mentoring, coaching, collegial – social and collegial – task. Means across the overall scale and subscales were well over the midpoint, ranging from $M = 3.32$ for coaching to 4.01 for collegial-task. The coaching subscale was the only scale or subscale to fall just short of the widely recognized .70 criteria for assessing a scale's reliability, so one should be cautious about generalizing findings on that subscale. An examination of differences in this scale and subdimensions by generation are presented below in Table 7.1.

There are no differences between generations and the main scale, as well as three of the four subscales. There is a significant difference in scores on Collegial – Task because Baby Boomers report significantly greater scores than both Gen X and Millennials.

The findings of our generational study are consistent with previous research, which indicates that there is not a generational difference when it comes to mentoring. This helps to underscore the importance of organizational mentoring, though, showcasing that everyone in an

Table 7.1 Generational Differences in the Mentoring and Communication Social Support Scale and Subscales

Measure	Baby Boomers M(SD)	Gen X M(SD)	Millennials M(SD)	F (2, 1147)	eta^2
Mentoring & Communication Social Support	3.69(.71)	3.64(.75)	3.67(.67)	.194	.00
Career Mentoring	3.41(.92)	3.51(.97)	3.60(.87)	2.432	.00
Coaching	3.20(1.03)	3.35(1.01)	3.31(.92)	.850	.00
Collegial – Social	3.77(.87)	3.61(95)	3.69(.86)	1.138	.00
Collegial – Task	**4.27(.80)**[a]	4.03(.89)[b]	3.97(.78)[b]	5.618*	.01

**$p < .001$, *$p < .05$.
[a,b]Significant differences between groups as determined by Tukey HSD post hocs. Scores that significantly differ from the other two scores are bolded.

organization can benefit from the process, regardless of whether they are the mentor or the mentee. Furthermore, with it comes to Baby Boomers, our data indicates that through mentoring, their feelings of social collegiality can improve, which is positive information that organizations should use as additional consideration for implementing mentorship initiatives. Finally, these findings demonstrate that mentoring represents one successful and positive prong in a larger program of supportive workplace programs and practices.

7.6 Best Practices for Creating a Supportive Multigenerational Workplace

The goal of a supportive workplace is to have happy, satisfied, and supported employees because when an organization's employees are happy, the benefits are endless, keeping the organization healthy. The following are some best practices that organizations can implement to improve support, but this is not an exhaustive list, and organizations are encouraged to regularly survey employees and conceptualize new ways to provide support.

Best Practice 1: Provide Enriching Experiences

According to a large workplace survey conducted by MetLife (2019), employees need an ally, and it does not need to be one specific person. Instead, employees need their organization to be their ally, and one way to do this is to provide enrichment opportunities that go beyond employee recognition, and instead, provide support. For instance, workplaces can offer workshops about financial topics or programs to reduce stress (lunchtime meditations, for example); encourage people to use their vacation time; and provide training so that people can do their job better and/or faster to support employees as both organizational assets and humans.

Best Practice 2: Listen

Listening is an important part of supportive communication and is free for organizations to implement. Supportive listening is characterized by focusing attention on the support seeker, expressing involvement, demonstrating understanding, and being both verbally and non-verbally responsive (Mikkola, 2019). In the workplace, anyone can be a supportive listener regardless of age, tenure, position, or power. The more that people engage in supportive listening, the more that people will communicate their needs for support, creating a cyclical process for support in the workplace.

Best Practice 3: Monitor Stress and Manage Uncertainty

There is not one workplace throughout the world where stress and uncertainty is nonexistent, regardless of how supportive the organizational culture is. Stress and uncertainty are workplace norms, but with that, supportive communication can also become a norm, as the concept is intimately linked with stress and uncertainty. One of the easiest ways to create and maintain a supportive work environment is to identify, monitor, and manage stress and uncertainty through communication. Simple tactics such as encouraging employees to discuss stressors and creating a shared need for support (on a project team, for instance) can provide support. Mikkola (2019) suggests reflecting on current communication practices and asking whether or not they promote supportive interactions. For instance, engaging in excessive and/or constant discussion of work and workplace problems can increase stress and lead to defensiveness in communication. Also, the practice of "rush talk" where people are constantly stating how busy and overworked they are promoting a culture of busyness and stress, which is not supportive and can hide communication efforts that seek support. Therefore, engaging in more supportive communication such as asking questions, having honest conversations, and acknowledging stress and uncertainty as hard and discomforting can promote supportive workplaces.

7.7 Conclusion

Similar to Chapter 5, which is about organizational culture, there are certain workplace practices that transcend age and are not influenced by generations. Supportive communication is another one of these items as demonstrated by our data. When a supportive workplace is present, generational effects are minimized, and people coexist with greater ease to help reach organizational goals. Therefore, promoting positive communication in the workplace can provide great benefits and help connect a multigenerational workforce.

References

Allen, T., Finkelstein, L., & Poteet, M. (2009). *Designing workplace mentoring programs: An evidence-based approach*. Wiley-Blackwell.

Bodie, G., & Burleson, B. (2008). Explaining variations in the effects of supportive messages: A dual-process framework. In C. Beck (Ed.), *Communication yearbook* (vol. *32*, pp. 354–398). Routledge.

Brashers, D. (2001). Communication and uncertainty management. *Journal of Communication, 15*, 477–497.

Burleson, B. (2003). Emotional support skills. In J. O. Green and B. Burleson (Eds.), *Handbook of communication and social interaction skills* (pp. 551–594). Lawrence Erlbaum.

Burleson, B. (2008). What counts as effective emotional support? Explorations of individual and situational differences. In M. T. Motley (Ed.), *Studies in applied interpersonal communication* (pp. 207–227). Sage.

Burleson, B. (2009). Understanding the outcomes of supportive communication: A dual-process approach. *Journal of Social and Personal Relationships, 26*, 21–38.

Burleson, B., & MacGeorge, E. (2002). Supportive communication. In M. L. Knapp & J. A. Daly (Eds.), *Handbook of interpersonal communication* (3rd ed., pp. 374–424). Sage.

Clark, R., Pierce, A., Finn, K., Hsu, K., Toosley, A., & Williams, L. (1998). The impact of alternative approaches to comforting, closeness of relationship, and gender on multiple measures of effectiveness. *Communication Studies, 49*, 224–239.

Cohen, S., Mermelstein, R., Karmarck, T., & Hoberman, H. (1985). Measuring the functional components of social support. In I. Sarason & B. Sarason (Eds.), *Social support: Theory, research, and applications* (pp. 73–94). Maritnus Nijhoff.

Cunningham, M., & Barbee, A. (2000). Social support. In C. Hendrick & S. Hendrick (Eds.), *Close relationships: A sourcebook* (pp. 272–285). Sage.

Cutrona, C., Cohen, B., & Igram, S. (1990). Contextual determinants of the perceived helpfulness of helping behaviors. *Journal of Social and Personal Relationships, 7*, 553–562.

Darling, L. (1985). What to do about toxic mentoring? *Journal of Nursing Administration, May 1985, 15*, 43–45.

Edge, K. (2014). A review of the empirical generations at work research: Implications for school leaders and future research. *School Leadership & Management, 34*, 136–155. https://doi.org/10.1080/13632434.2013.869206

Feeley, T., Moon, D., Kozey, R., & Lowe, A. (2010). An erosion model of employee turnover based on network centrality. *Journal of Applied Communication Research, 38*, 167–188.

Feng, B. (2009). Testing an integrated model of advice-giving in supportive interactions. *Human Communication Research, 35*, 115–129.

Glynn, L., Christenfeld, N., & Gerin, W. (1999). Gender, social support, and cardiovascular responses to stress. *Psychosomatic Medicine, 61*, 234–242.

Gottlieb, B. (1994). Social support. In A. Weber & J. Harvey (Eds.), *Perspectives on close relationships* (pp. 307–324). Allyn & Bacon.

Greengard, S. (2002). Moving forward with reverse mentoring. *Workforce, March*, 15.

Grunig, J., & Grunig, L. (2008). Excellence theory in public relations: Past, present, and future. In A. Zerfass, B. van Ruler, & K. Sriramesh (Eds.), *Public relations research: European and international perspectives and innovations* (pp. 327–347). VS Verlag.

Harris, J., Winskowski, A., & Engdahl, B. (2007). Types of workplace social support in the prediction of job satisfaction. *The Career Development Quarterly, 56*, 150–156.

Harvey, M., & Buckley, M. (2002). Assessing the "conventional wisdoms" of management for the 21st Century organization. *Organizational Dynamics, 30*, 368–378.

Hewlett, S., Sherbin, L., & Sumberg, K. (2009). Let GenY teach you. Retrieved from https://hbr.org/2009/06/let-gen-y-teach-you-tech

Hill, S. E., Bahniuk, M. H., Dobos, J., & Rouner, D. (1989). Mentoring and other communication support in the academic setting. *Group and Organization Studies, 14*, 355–368. doi: 10.1177/105960118901400308

Jacobi, M. (1991). Mentoring and undergraduate academic success: A literature review. *Review of Educational Research, 61*, 505–532.

Jacobson, D. (1986). Types and timing of social support. *Journal of Health and Social Behavior, 27*, 250–264.

Kogler Hill, S., & Gant, G. (2000). Mentoring by minorities for minorities: The organizational support system. *Review of Business, 21*, 53–57.

Lambert, E., Minor, K., Wells, J., & Hogan, N. (2016). Social support's relationship to correctional staff job stress, job involvement, job satisfaction, and organizational commitment. *Social Science Journal, 53*, 22–32.

Levinson, D., Darrow, C., Klein, E., Levinson, M., & McKeen, B. (1978). *Seasons of a man's life*. Knopf.

MacGeorge, E., Feng, B., & Thompson, E. (2008). "Good" and "bad" advice: How to advise more effectively. In M. Motley (Ed.), *Studies in applied interpersonal communication* (pp. 145–164). Sage.

MetLife (2019). Thriving in the new work-life world. MetLife's 17th annual U.S. employee benefit trends study. Retrieved from https://www.metlife.com/content/dam/metlifecom/us/ebts/pdf/MetLife-Employee-Benefit-Trends-Study-2019.pdf

Mikkola, L. (2019). Supportive communication in the workplace. In L. Mikkola & M. Valo (Eds.), *Workplace communication* (pp. 147–162). Taylor & Francis.

Murphy, W. (2012). Reverse mentoring at work: Fostering cross-generational learning and developing Millennial leaders. *Human Resource Management, 51*, 549–574.

Neff, L., & Karney, B. (2005). Gender differences in social support: A question of skill or responsiveness? *Journal of Personality and Social Psychology, 7*, 561–570.

Park, K., Wilson, M., & Lee, M. (2004). Effects of social support at work on depression and organizational productivity. *American Journal of Health Behavior, 28*, 444–455.

Prehm, H., & Iscson, S. (1985). Mentorship: Student and faculty perspectives. *Teacher Education and Special Education: The Journal of the Teacher Education Division of the Council for Exceptional Children, 8*, 12–16.

Sambunjak, D., Straus, S., & Marusic, A. (2009). A systematic review of qualitative research on the meaning and characteristics of mentoring in academic medicine. *Journal of General Internal Medicine, 25*, 72–78.

Sands, R., Parson, L., & Duane, J. (1991). Faculty mentoring faculty in a public university. *The Journal of Higher Education, 62*, 174–193.

Shaver, P. (2008, Spring). Some necessary links between communication studies and social psychology in research on close relationships. *Relationship Research News, 6*, 1–2.

Singh, A., Singh, A., & Singhi, N. (2015). Organizational role stress and social support as predictors of job satisfaction among managerial personnel. *Journal of Social Service Research, 40*, 178–188.

Snyder, J. (2009). The role of coworker and supervisor social support in alleviating the experience of burnout for caregivers in the human-services industry. *Southern Communication Journal, 74*, 373–389.

Uno, D., Uchino, B., & Smith, T. (2002). Relationship quality moderates the effect of social support given by close friends on cardiovascular reactivity in women. *International Journal of Behavioral Medicine, 9*, 243–262.

Young, A., & Perrewe, P. (2000). What did you expect? An examination of career-related support and social support among mentors and proteges. *Journal of Management, 26*, 611–632.

8   The Dark Side of Communication at Work: Conflict and Dissent

This chapter will explore destructive workplace communication – specifically, conflict and dissent. The authors will reflect on their findings and connect these findings to previous literature surrounding conflict and dissent. This chapter will address multigenerational workplace preferences, including crisis communication in the work environment.

8.1 Ineffective Communication in the Workplace

In an ideal world, employees would understand supervisor expectations clearly, tasks would be accurately completed, and workplace relationships would be positive and supportive. Unfortunately, our world is not idealistic, and often workplaces struggle to create an environment that is conducive to positive communication. Indeed, communication is crucial to organizational structures, with Odine (2015) even remarking that management can only thrive in the prevalence of communication. A positive and supportive communication climate does not happen naturally and instead must be nurtured and developed. Our organizations are, probably, more likely to engage in and practice ineffective communication.

In 2011, Chandra, Theng, Lwin, and Shou-Boon (2011) identified uncertainty as one of the primary barriers to effective communication in the workplace. The concept of uncertainty tends to lead to equivocality or ambiguity. These barriers are more conceptual, relying on the message and the sender. Other barriers exist, including cultural and language differences; literal physical barriers that impact noise; psychological barriers like self-esteem, jargon, and language; differing expectations; or even differing abilities. This list is nowhere near exhaustive. Yet, despite all of these challenges, for organizations to truly develop an environment where employees want to work and to avoid significant turnover (Nwagbara, Oruh, Ugorji, & Ennsra, 2013), communication should be a key component of an organization's mission. Ineffective communication can lead to decreased productivity, satisfaction, and lower retention rates (Salahuddin, 2010).

In some ways, ineffective communication may also boil down to employee expectations. Millennials, for one, prefer organizations that have a reduced hierarchical structure (Barnes, 2009). For this group, then, communication in the workplace that is ineffective would seem to reinforce "red tape" or decrease transparency. While this is not the only communication difference between generations, it is prevalent.

A deteriorating focus on communication can have significant ramifications beyond those traditionally reserved for job functionality. Specifically, ineffective communication can become inherently negative. Workplace bullying, for one, can occur because of diminished communication channels (Venkataramani, Labianca, & Grosser, 2013). Gossip can also occur when communication expectations have not been defined clearly (Ye, Zhu, Deng, & Mu, 2019). These consequences highlight the dark side of workplace communication, but there are other manifestations of negative communication in the workplace as well.

8.2 Manifestations of Negative Communication

Just because communication is ineffective does not mean it is inherently negative. In fact, ambiguity in some cases does not manifest itself as either a positive or negative outcome. Instead, it could occur because of poor planning or basic misunderstanding. Yet, there are instances where communication in the workplace becomes a negative event with negative results. Negative messages cause unpleasant reactions even as intense as sickness, absences, reduced motivation, and productivity declines leading to financial consequences (Kline & Lewis, 2019). Generally, negative communication leads to negative relationships in the workplace (Keashly & Jagatic, 2003). Workers, struggling to control a negative communication environment, will see increased stress, emotional load, turnover, and cynicism toward the organization and their life in general (Fritz & Omdahl, 2006). Negative communicative behaviors can be long-lasting affairs or isolated incidents. No matter the duration, negative behaviors can lead to long-term emotional strain.

Negative communicative behaviors and problematic relationships can manifest through different relational categorizations. Tuikka (2020) believes the most problematic negative relationships in the workplace are those that are uncivil, aggressive, (sexually) harassing, unwanted, or are defined by conduct that is unprofessional. Organizations should clearly identify their expectations for handling unethical, uncivil, and unprofessional communication (Fritz, 2019).

Uncivil Relationships

Incivility is pervasive in organizations (Cortina & Magley, 2009). While the definition of incivility, especially in the workplace, is somewhat ambiguous (Andersson & Pearson, 1999), it is important to note that there is some form of deviance or violated norms for respect associated with incivility. Incivility may be spurred on by many factors, but perceived intent to harm may be one of the most influential factors that contributes to employee mistreatment. No matter what the reasons, organizations should determine that civility will be a central tenet of their culture.

Harassment

Harassment, especially sexual harassment, is widespread (Hardies, 2019). McDonald (2012) defines sexual harassment as behaviors toward targets and can include unwanted sexual comments, propositions or requests, gestures, or even actions and assault. Like other negative communication, sexual harassment can lead to mental and physical health challenges and decreased job performance (Willness, Steel, & Lee, 2007).

Incivility and harassment can generally be classified as behavior that is unprofessional. Unprofessional behavior, and negative communication, fuel dysfunctional organizational culture. And, especially because there are now additional outlets, like social media platforms, for these dark side behaviors to occur, organizations would be wise to address their policies and procedures related to these actions.

Unfortunately, organizations that struggle to handle this dark side of workplace communication may struggle to adapt and evolve in an environment increasingly concerned with positive and supportive climates. As virtual work has become more prominent, tasks that at one time were completed face to face are now completed in computer-mediated environments (Vrankes, Bailien, Vandebosch, Erreygers, & De Witte, 2017). Organizations, therefore need to focus not only on negative communication in physical contexts but also on negative or damaging communication in virtual environments. All of this to say: ignoring the dark side of workplace communication is not a luxury the 21st century organization can afford. Negative communication has far-reaching effects. For our purposes, though, two of the most pressing consequences of negative communication include conflict and dissent.

8.3 Conflict

8.3.1 Previous Research and Theory

Conflict in the workplace is inevitable and occurs in all organizations (Tuikka, 2020). However, the actual manifestation of conflict, and for our purposes the analysis of conflict in the workplace, can be an area of disagreement (Chaudry & Asif, 2015). No matter how conflict in organizations comes to fruition, it has been a significant area of study for researchers (Litterer, 1966).

The definition of conflict is debated. The range of different definitions conceptualizes conflict as a reflection of interpersonal hostility (Barki & Hartwick, 2001), a phenomenon that includes emotions, perceptions, and behaviors (Pondy, 1969), or even disagreement of how to achieve certain goals Jehn, 1997). Chaudry and Asif (2015) believe the common theme of these varying definitions revolves around identifying what triggers and prolongs conflict. They, then, conceptualize conflict as a "cohesive framework of behavior and perception of organizational members, which is triggered by the feelings of being deprived with an awareness of incompatibility with others" (Chaudry & Asif, 2015, p. 239). This definition is helpful because it brings to light a condition where conflict arises because one does not get what they want or finds a relationship incompatible.

Like the actual definition of conflict itself, expert opinions differ on the benefits of conflict. Some view conflict as a functional dynamic (Chen, 2006; Harolds & Woods, 2006; Jehn & Bendersky, 2003), while others view conflict as damaging to the organizational structure (De Dreu, 2008; Litterer, 1966). Recognizing that individual situations and organizations probably have different outcomes related to their conflict, it is worth noting that the results of conflict probably depend more on organizational culture and personal relationships within the organization and are not necessarily inherently positive or negative (Sharma & Singh, 2019). Ultimately, individuals in organizations will handle conflict differently.

From a generational perspective, Dencker, Joshi, and Martocchio, 2008 believe that an accurate understanding of generational differences in the workplace that help mitigate conflict and enhance conflict resolution. Conflict can occur in workplaces between generations for a variety of reasons. Urick, Hollensbe, and Masterson (2012) identify three different forms of intergenerational conflict: value based, behavior based, and identity based. Intergenerational work conflict can occur because of several different factors but miscommunication, work-life balance, technology-use differences (Carver & Candela, 2008), and issues with older/younger supervisor dyadic relationship challenges (Collins, Hair, & Rocco, 2009). Unfortunately, if not handled properly, generational conflict in the workplace can negatively impact the organization (Sessa, Kabacoff, Deal, & Brown, 2007).

To measure conflict in organizations, Putnam and Wilson (1982) developed the Organizational Communication Conflict Instrument (OCCI). Their instrument, unlike those prior, focuses on concrete communicative behaviors, not just conflict styles. We used this measure to identify generational differences in endorsements of various conflict strategies in the workplace. Their instrument asked participants how often they use a particular strategy. Specifically, their strategies were nonconfrontation strategies (generally avoid disagreements, downplaying controversies, or approaching conflict indirectly); solutions-oriented strategies (using compromise or a search for innovation); and finally control strategies (those behaviors that seek to manage conflict by arguing for particular positions). These three subdimensions help to inform our understanding of how employees engage in actual communication behaviors related to conflict.

8.3.2 Conflict and Generational Differences: Our Data

The Organizational Communication Conflict Instrument (Putnam & Wilson, 1982) was used to index endorsement of three different conflict strategies: Nonconfrontation, solutions-oriented, and control strategies. The scale and its three subscales all demonstrated reliability coefficients > .82. Greater numbers on this (7-point) scale indicate greater agreement that individuals adopt each of the three strategies, where Solutions-oriented strategies has the greatest average, $M = 4.77$, $SD = .94$), followed by nonconfrontation strategies ($M = 3.97$, $SD = 1.13$) and lastly control strategies ($M = 3.25$, $SD = 1.13$). An analysis of differences across the three generations is presented in Table 8.1.

Results show overall similar endorsement of each of the three strategies, with significant differences emerging in nonconfrontation strategies. Here, we see Millennials endorse this strategy to a greater extent than both Gen X and Baby Boomers.

8.4 Dissent

8.4.1 Previous Research and Theory

Conflict can, potentially, lead to organizational dissent. Dissent, according to Kassing (1998), is "how employees verbally express their

Table 8.1 Generational Differences in the Organizational Communication Conflict Instrument and Subscales

Measure	Baby Boomers M(SD)	Gen X M(SD)	Millennials M(SD)	F (2, 1147)	eta^2
Organizational Com. Conflict Instrument	3.93(.65)[a]	3.95(.63)[a]	**4.15(.63)[b]**	12.432**	.02
Non-Confrontation Strategies	3.64(1.15)[a]	3.74(1.22)[a]	**4.07(1.09)[b]**	12.454**	.02
Solutions-Oriented Strategies	4.79(.98)	4.66(1.02)	4.81(.91)	2.262	.00
Control Strategies	3.10(1.11)	3.20(1.17)	3.28(1.13)	1.201	.00

**$p < .001$, *$p < .05$.
[a,b]Significant differences between groups as determined by Tukey HSD post hocs. Scores that significantly differ from the other two scores are bolded.

contradictory opinions and disagreements about organizational phenomena" (p. 183). Dissent, then, manifests in the sharing of employee opinions about the organization. As one can imagine, a negative communication climate can lead to high levels of organizational dissent. Theoretically dissent is expressed when employees, specifically, share "contradictory opinions about organizational practices, policies, and operations" (Kassing, 1998, p. 183).

Generational differences surrounding dissent and the expression of dissent in organizations tend to vary. For instance, Shakil and Siddiqui (2020) report that when millennials are unable to express their dissent, the situation becomes more detrimental, especially to their sense of commitment to the organization. Boomers, on the other hand, tend to be a little more positive related to their overall work values and report that they view work as an extension of their self-interests and as a place where they can experience gratification and growth (Zemke, Raines, & Filipczak, 1999). Gen Xers tend to represent the opposite end of the spectrum. Members of Generation X spent their formative years in organizations where downsizing and outsourcing were common practices (Jones & Murray, 2019). Ironically, Millennials tend to have higher levels of overall company satisfaction compared to Xers (Kowske, Rasch, & Wiley, 2010) yet Millennials are more inclined to communicate their dissenting thoughts to coworkers and supervisors (Myers & Sadaghiani, 2010). These realities create a difficult communication environment for employees and supervisors to navigate.

One way organizations can create a safe environment for employees to share organizational feedback is by recognizing how dissent is communicated in their organization. To measure organizational dissent, Kassing (2000), developed an 18-item Organizational Dissent Scale, which indexes overall dissent toward the organization along two different sub-dimensions: articulated and latent.

Articulated Dissent

Employees who believe their dissent will be perceived more favorably tend to practice articulated dissent. In instances where articulated dissent is expressed, employees assume their thoughts will be perceived as helpful or constructive and that the hearers will not retaliate against the employee who voices the concern (Kassing, 1997). Employees, too, who express their dissent in this way tend to communicate to those who they believe can actually make some change.

Latent Dissent

Unlike articulated dissent, latent dissent, originally conceptualized as antagonistic dissent, tends to be more adversarial. Those who express latent dissent tend to believe they are still safe from retaliation because they possess an organizational leverage (Kassing, 1997). The term latent dissent also expresses a nonobservable concept meaning, dissent readily exists but may not be easy to measure or observe, and as the dissent grows, the possibility for observation tends to increase.

Workplace communication, specifically negative workplace communication, has substantial implications on day-to-day operations and productivity. Even in "normal" workplace scenarios, it can be hard to manage so many personalities, relationships, and generational differences. Yet, in crisis situations, organizations should work even harder to create environments that are transparent and effective. To combat negative communication in crisis that leads to conflict and dissent, organizations should develop a strategy that clearly identifies a crisis communication strategy and different ideas for communication in a multigenerational workplace during crisis situations.

Table 8.2 Generational Differences in the Organizational Dissent Scale and Subscales

Measure	Baby Boomers M(SD)	Gen X M(SD)	Millennials M(SD)	F (2, 1147)	eta^2
Organizational Dissent Scale	2.94(.58)	3.03(.68)	3.02(.58)	.893	.00
Articulated Dissent	**2.37(.74)**[a]	**2.66(.86)**[b]	**2.86(.82)**[c]	17.809**	.03
Latent Dissent	3.50(.84)[a]	3.40(.911)[a]	**3.18(.70)**[b]	13.619**	.02

**p < .001, *p < .05.
[a,b]Significant differences between groups as determined by Tukey HSD post hocs. Scores that significantly differ from the other two scores are bolded.

8.4.2 Dissent and Generational Differences: Our Data

Kassing's (2000) Organizational Dissent Scale demonstrated reliability (Cronbach's alpha = .824). Across all participants, scores were higher for Latent Dissent (*M* = 3.25, *SD* = .77) than for Articulated Dissent (*M* = 2.78, *SD* = .83), on a 5-point scale. Analyses of differences across generations are presented in Table 8.2.

Interesting, significant differences are found across articulated and latent dissent among the generations. Notably, Millennials stick out as demonstrating the *greatest* articulated dissent and the *least* latent dissent. This finding reflects previous research that Millennials are more likely to be more vocal about their dissent in the workplace. The opposite pattern is true for Baby Boomers, who show the least articulated dissent and the greatest latent dissent (although they do not differ from nearly as low Gen X in latent dissent).

8.5 Multigenerational Crisis Response

In organizations, as employers struggle to overcome negative communication, conflict, and dissent, a firm grasp of crisis management is also important for the modern manager. Crisis researchers have primarily focused on external messaging in crisis situations (Frandsen & Johansen, 2011), but internal stakeholders need crisis leadership as well. And, in our modern organizations where incivility, harassment, bullying, and other dark side interactions are common, a crisis approach can be helpful. Crisis situations, referred by Mitroff (2005) as major acts of betrayal, should be approached with wisdom and intentionally. In turn, employers should strive for an element of transparency as they deal with internal crisis situations. Transparency, according to Schnackenberg and Tomlinson (2016), is the "perceived quality of intentionally shared information from a sender" (p. 1788). A transparency initiative will speak volumes to Millennials and Generation Z. As Stewart, Oliver, Cravens, and Oishi (2017) point out, increased transparency can help increase an employee's drive and increase operational efficiency.

External relationships tend to drive crisis communication; however, as a potential categorization of negative or dark-side internal communication, crises can be approached similarly to other employee communication. Strategic communication between managers and internal stakeholders should, generally, promote commitment and organizational belonging (Welch, 2012).

Historically, research has conceptualized crisis communication based on which channels are utilized and/or how frequently messaging occurs; however, this approach may fall short of what organizations actually need to know and share about their internal crisis strategy (Ruck & Welch, 2012). While it is important to consider both frequency and channel in crisis situations, the actual content and the impending dialogue brought about by messages should be a focal point of employers. However, channels used to communicate in crisis situations should be adaptable and, from a generational perspective, managers must be more adept today at using technology to respond to crisis situations in organizations (Vielhaber & Waltman, 2008) because new or efficient technologies can be used to communicate with different generational groups, and younger generations prefer high-tech channels.

8.6 Best Practices for Handling Conflict, Dissent, and Crisis in the Modern Multigenerational Organization

The consideration of employers and managers, when dealing with all that goes into the dark side of corporate communication, is a topic not for the faint of heart. The institutional ramifications of negative communication, including but limited to conflict and dissent, as well as potential crisis situations should be approached thoughtfully. To offer practical solutions or guidance for dealing with negative communication in the workplace, the following best practices are proposed.

Best Practice 1: Establish a Culture of Advocacy and when Necessary, Appropriate Policies

Organizations must work to establish an organizational culture that emphasizes equitability, advocacy, and inclusion. Along those lines, establishing a culture where people understand how to be in re-lationships with each other can create a tone of positive normalcy. Meaning, positive interaction can become the norm not the exception. However, to do this, it may be appropriate to establish policies for behavior that is unacceptable. When you communicate clearly to your people that bullying, harassment, and other manifestations of negative communication will not be tolerated, it can shed light on your orga-nizational values. In addition, clarifying for your people how to deal with conflict and dissent, giving appropriate time and context for disagreement, can also be helpful. In sum, normalize the process for healthy conflict and dissent and formalize a policy against unhealthy negative communication and behavior.

Best Practice 2: Be Transparent (When You Can)

From a generational perspective, transparency can be a nonnegotiable desire for Millennials and members of Generation Z. Generation X and Baby Boomers have less demanding expectations for transparency and accountability from their bosses and supervisors, but they still desire open and appropriate communication. Be transparent when you can. Let your people know how you are dealing with internal crises, inform them of your rationale for decisions, and communicate information that they need to know. Obviously, you cannot be transparent about everything, but ask yourself if you are sharing everything you should share.

Best Practice 3: Do not Allow Dissent to Fester

Employees will always have dissenting opinions. However, pretending that employees are on board with every decision and that they do not need a chance to share their perspective can lead to a dangerous outcome. Dissent can be helpful because it provides additional action steps and differentiated operations. Do not be afraid of dissent or conflict, but make sure you have identified your own personal style for dealing with both then provide opportunities for healthy feedback. Ignoring dissenting opinions or failing to provide opportunities for employees to share differing thoughts in a safe space can allow dissent to fester and become a negative cultural distinction. Generally, people appreciate the opportunity to share their thoughts, and younger gen-erations in particular – those more willing to be explicit about their opinions – will generally take you up on opportunities you provide. As you think about a platform for employee sharing, determine if the feedback should be anonymous, think about follow-up mechanisms, and provide clear communication about how feedback will be received. Clearly communicate a cycle for feedback and follow-up.

8.7 Conclusion

Our data show an interesting parallel to previous research. For one, Millennials are not afraid to voice their concerns and opinions, as they relate to the workplace. This new cultural dimension, one of unabashed vocal feedback and opinion sharing, is relatively new and was not a sustained characteristic of Gen X or Boomer employees. In addition, we see, ironically, Millennials appreciate nonconfrontational strategies when dealing with workplace conflict. This particular group, those Generation Y (i.e. Millennials) workers, again show a new and unique way of dealing with issues and challenges in the modern work environment.

References

Andersson, L. M., & Pearson, C. M. (1999). Tit for tat? The spiraling effect of incivility in the workplace. *Academy of Management Review*, *24*, 452–471.

Barki, H., & Hartwick, J. (2001). Interpersonal conflict and its management in information system development. *MIS Quarterly*, *25*, 195–228.

Barnes, G. (2009). Guess who's coming to work: Generation Y. Are you ready for them? *Public Library Quarterly*, *28*, 60.

Carver, L., & Candela, L. (2008). Attaining organizational commitment across different generations of nurses. *Journal of Nursing Management*, *16*, 984–991. doi: 10.1111/j.1365-2834.2008.00911.x

Chandra, S., Theng, Y., Lwin, M. O., & Shou-Boon, S. (2011, May 26–30). *Exploring trust to reduce communication barriers in virtual world collaborations* [paper]. 60th Annual International Communication Association (ICA) Conference, Boston. https://www.researchgate.net/profile/May_Lwin/publication/267381074_Exploring_Trust_to_Reduce_Communication_Barriers_in_Virtual_World_Collaborations/links/5474abb10cf2778985abf047.pdf

Chaudry, A. M., & Asif, R. (2015). Organizational conflict and conflict management: A synthesis of literature. *Journal of Business and Management Research*, *9*, 238–244.

Chen, M. H. (2006). Understanding the benefits and detriments of conflict on team creativity process. *Creativity and Innovation Management*, *15*, 105–116.

Collins, M., Hair, J., & Rocco, T. (2009). The older-worker-younger-supervisor dyad: A test of the reverse Pygmalion effect. *Human Resource Development Quarterly*, *20*, 21–41. doi: 10.1002/hrdq.20006

Cortina, L. M., & Magley, V. J. (2009). Patterns and profiles of response to incivility in the workplace. *Journal of Occupational Health Psychology*, *14*, 272–288.

De Dreu, C. K. (2008). The virtue and vice of workplace conflict: Food for (pessimistic) thought. *Journal of Organizational Behavior, 29,* 5–18.

Dencker, J. C., Joshi, A., & Martocchio, J. J. (2008). Towards a theoretical framework linking generational memories to workplace attitudes and behaviors. *Human Resource Management Review, 18,* 180–187.

Frandsen, F., & Johansen, W. (2011). The study of internal crisis communication: Towards an integrative framework. *Corporate Communications: An International Journal, 16,* 347–361. https://doi.org/10.1108/13563281111186977

Fritz, J. M. H. (2019). Communicating ethics and bullying. In R. West & C. S. Beck (Eds.), *The Routledge handbook of communication and bullying* (pp. 22–29). Routledge.

Fritz, J. M. H., & Omdahl, B. L. (2006). *Problematic relationships in the workplace.* Peter Lang.

Hardies, K. (2019). Personality, social norms, and sexual harassment in the workplace. *Personality and Individual Differences, 151,* 1–5. https://doi.org/10.1016/j.paid.2019.07.006

Harolds, J., & Wood, B. P. (2006). Conflict management and resolution. *Journal of the American College of Radiology, 3,* 200–206.

Jehn, K. A. (1997). A qualitative analysis of conflict types and dimensions in organizational groups. *Administrative Science Quarterly, 42,* 530–557.

Jehn, K. A., & Bendersky, C. (2003). Intragroup conflict in organizations: A contingency perspective on the conflict outcome relationship. *Research in Organizational Behavior, 25,* 187–242.

Jones, J. S., & Murray, S. R. (2019). The effect of generational differences on work values and attitudes. *International Journal of Research in Business and Management, 1,* 25–35.

Kassing, J. W. (1997). Articulating, agonizing, and displacing: A model of employee dissent. *Communication Studies, 48,* 311–331.

Kassing, J. W. (1998). Development and validation of the organizational dissent scale. *Management Communication Quarterly, 12,* 183–229.

Kassing, J. W. (2000). Investigating the relationship between superior-subordinate relationship quality and employee dissent. *Communication Research Reports, 17,* 58–70.

Keashly, L., & Jagatic, K. (2003). By any other name: American perspectives on workplace bullying. In E. Einarsen, H. Hoel, D. Zapf, & Cooper, C., Eds., *Bullying and emotional abuse in the workplace: International perspectives in research and practice* (pp. 31–36). Taylor & Francis.

Kline, R., & Lewis, D. (2019). The price of fear: Estimating the financial cost of bullying and harassment to the NHS in England. *Public Money and Management, 39,* 166–174.

Kowske, B., Rasch, R., & Wiley, J. (2010). Millennials' (lack of) attitude problem: An empirical examination of generational effects on work attitudes. *Journal of Business & Psychology, 25,* 265–279

Litterer, J. A. (1966). Conflict in organization: A reexamination. *Academy of Management Journal, 9,* 178–186.

McDonald, P. (2012). Workplace sexual harassment 30 years on: A review of the literature. *International Journal of Management Reviews, 14,* 1–17.

Mitroff, I.I. (2005). *Why some companies emerge stronger and better from a crisis.* Amacom.

Myers, K., & Sadaghiani, K. (2010). Millennials in the workplace: A communication perspective on Millennials' organizational relationships and performance. *Journal of Business & Psychology, 25,* 225–238.

Nwagbara, U., Oruh, E. S., Ugorji, C., & Ennsra, M. (2013). The impact of effective communication on employee turnover intension at First Bank of Nigeria, *4,* 13–21.

Odine, M. (2015). Communication problems in management. *Journal of Emerging Issues in Economics, Finance and Banking, 4,* 1615–1630.

Pondy, L. R. (1969). Varieties of organizational conflict. *Administrative Science Quarterly, 14,* 499–505.

Putnam, L. L., & Wilson, C. E. (1982). Communicative strategies in organizational conflicts: Reliability and validity of a measurement scale. *Communication Yearbook, 6,* 629–652.

Ruck, K., & Welch, M. (2012). Valuing internal communication: Management and employee perspectives. *Public Relations Review, 38,* 294–302. doi:10.1016/j.pubrev.2011.12.016

Salahuddin, M. M. (2010). Generational differences impact on leadership style and organizational success. *Journal of Diversity Management, 5,* 1–6. https://doi.org/10.19030/jdm.v5i2.805

Schnackenberg, A. K., & Tomlinson, E. C. (2016). Organizational transparency: A new perspective on managing trust in organization-stakeholder relationships. *Journal of Management, 42*(7), 1784–1810. doi: 10.1177/0149206314525202

Sessa, V., Kabacoff, R., Deal, J., & Brown, H. (2007). Research tools for the psychologist-manager: Generational differences in leader values and leadership behaviors. *Psychologist-Manager Journal, 10,* 47–74. doi: 10.1080/10887.150701205543

Shakil, B., & Siddiqui, D. A. (2020). Factors affecting millennials employees' dissent and its subsequent impact on their commitment. Retrieved from https://ssrn.com/abstract=3683231

Sharma, S., & Singh, K. (2019). Positive organizational culture: Conceptualizing managerial role in interpersonal conflict. *European Journal of Business & Social Sciences, 7,* 1508–1518.

Stewart, J. S., Oliver, E. G., Cravens, K. S., & Oishi, S. (2017). Managing millennials: Embracing generational differences. *Business Horizons, 60,* 45–54. https://doi.org/10.1016/j.bushor.2016.08.011

Tuikka, S. (2020). Negative relationships in the workplace. In L. Mikkola & M. Valo (Eds.), *Workplace communication.* Routledge.

Urick, M. J., Hollensbe, E. C., & Masterson, S. S. (2012). Understanding and managing generational tensions. Presented at Academy of Management Annual Meeting, Boston, MA.

Venkataramani, V., Labianca, G. J., & Grosser, T. (2013). Positive and ne-gative workplace relationships, social satisfaction, and organizational at-tachment. *Journal of Applied Psychology, 98*(6), 1028–1039. https://doi.org/10.1037/a0034090

Vielhaber, M. E., & Waltman, J. L. (2008). Changing uses of technology: Crisis communication responses in a faculty strike. *The Journal of Business Communication (1973), 45*(3), 308–330.

Vrankes, I., Bailien, E., Vandebosch, H., Erreygers, S., & De Witte, H. (2017). The dark side of working online: Towards a definition and an emotion re-action model of workplace cyberbullying. *Computer in Human Behavior, 69*, 324–334. https://doi.org/10.1016/j.chb.2016.12.055

Welch, M. (2012). Appropriateness and acceptability: Employee perspectives of internal communication. *Public Relations Review, 38*, 246–254. doi:10.1016/j.pubrev.2011.12.017

Willness, C. R., Steel, P., & Lee, K. (2007). A meta-analysis of the antecedents and consequences of workplace sexual harassment. *Personnel Psychology, 60*, 127–162.

Ye, Y., Zhu, H., Deng, X., & Mu, Z. (2019). Negative workplace gossip and service outcomes: An explanation from social identity theory. *International Journal of Hospitality Management, 82*, 159–168. https://doi.org/10.1016/j.ijhm.2019.04.020

Zemke, R., Raines, C., & Filipczak, B. (1999). *Generations at work: Managing the class of veterans, boomers, Xers, and nexters in your workplace.* AMACOM.

9 Workplace Satisfaction

This chapter focuses on generational perspectives on workplace satisfaction.

9.1 Communication and Workplace Satisfaction

Extensive research on the relationship between communication satisfaction, first conceptualized by Downs and Hazen (1977), and job satisfaction did not begin until the mid-1970s (Pincus, 1986). Since that time, communication satisfaction has become a stable construct in organizational communication research (Crino & White, 1981). However, more than two decades ago, Pincus (1986) noted the lack of research examining the relationships between communication satisfaction, job satisfaction, and communication channel. Surprisingly, given the rapidly expanding capabilities of communication technologies, research in this area is still developing, and with the changes of 2020, this will remain a hot topic within empirical organizational research and for organizations.

Within the organizational setting, communication satisfaction is defined as "an individual's satisfaction with various aspects of communication in his organization" (Crino & White, 1981, pp. 831–832). Akkirman and Harris (2005) measured the following six factors: employees' relationship with supervisor, communication climate, overall communication satisfaction, horizontal communication, organizational integration, and personal feedback. The researchers discovered that teleworkers experience higher levels of communication satisfaction on all factors compared to traditional office workers. Tsai and Chuang (2009) found that supervisory communication, personal feedback, and communication climate are the greatest contributors to the communication-job performance relationship among employees. Although these two studies investigated the broader organizational communication structures, past research has not significantly accounted for the role of interpersonal communication satisfaction and job satisfaction among employees.

Interpersonal communication satisfaction within the workplace can be defined as "an employee's overall affective reaction to his or her evaluation of interaction patterns with coworkers across situations and levels within an organization" (Park & Raile, 2010, p. 572). Interpersonal relationships play a significant role in the satisfaction of employees as it relates to various constructs including communication satisfaction. Informal co-worker interactions are important for building synergy within the organization (Kurland & Bailey, 1999). In addition, satisfying interpersonal relationships are crucial for effective performance and the spreading of organizational culture (Watson-Manheim & Belanger, 2007). Furthermore, research has found the necessity of physical proximity in the development of co-worker relationships to be the least important factor for communication satisfaction (Sias, Pedersen, Gallagher, & Kopaneva, 2012).

It is challenging to separate communication satisfaction from job satisfaction because the two concepts are so related. However, typically if someone is very dissatisfied with their job, it relates back to a communication issue, indicating that communication satisfaction is an antecedent to job satisfaction. There are exceptions to this, of course, but understanding communication satisfaction independently before exploring job satisfaction can help discern when communication is going well and when communication practices need work so as not to disrupt a person's overall job satisfaction.

9.1.1 Previous Research and Theory

Two theories from previous research can help explain workplace communication satisfaction; employers will find these theories useful, especially when it comes to understanding the preferences of a multigenerational workforce. Understanding these two theories can help prevent miscommunications and communication dissatisfaction with a multigenerational workforce, leading to more effective communication and better outcomes among employees. The two theories are: media richness theory and channel expansion theory, which are commonly studied together.

Media Richness Theory

Media richness theory has emerged as one of the most widely studied and cited frameworks in the body of research on organizational media use (D'Urso & Rains, 2008). The premise of media richness theory is that a communication medium should be consistent with the needs of the message for effective communication (Lengel & Daft, 1988). Richness concerns a medium's capacity to convey various types of information cues in a manner that approximates face-to-face communication (Sheer, 2011). Media richness follows a continuum from high richness (i.e. face-to-face) to low richness (i.e. bulletin boards) for understanding the transmission of messages. The richness of a medium comprises four aspects: (1) the availability of instant feedback, which allows questions to be asked and answered; (2) the use of multiple cues, such as physical presence, vocal inflection, body gestures, words, numbers, and graphic symbols; (3) the use of natural language, which can be used to convey an understanding of a broad set of concepts and ideas; and (4) the personal focus of the medium (Lengel & Daft, 1988). When none or only a few of these attributes are present, a medium is considered "lean" (Sheer, 2011). Therefore, face-to-face is considered the richest medium because it allows for all four aspects important in communication.

The most effective choice of media is one that matches the intended outcome for a message, which indicates whether a rich or lean media should be utilized for message distribution (Easton & Bommelje, 2011). Sheer and Chen (2004) demonstrated that rich media have greater personal information-carrying capacities than lean media as analogous to communication immediacy. Additional research has favored face-to-face communication, pointing out that humans are most accustomed to "natural" characteristics only present in face-to-face communication (Kock, 2004) and that face-to-face interactions hold social advantages not present in other forms of media communications (Green et al., 2005).

According to the theory, messages should be communicated on channels with appropriate richness capabilities. When information is communicated using an inappropriate channel, the information is likely to be misinterpreted or seen as ineffective with regard to the intended purpose (Carlson & Zmud, 1999). Additionally, when a message and medium mismatch occurs, communication parties have to engage in compensating communication activities, which takes additional time and resources (Hollingshead, McGrath, & O'Connor, 1993). Media richness research has spent a considerable amount of time identifying the limitations of one channel versus others. For example, Jacobsen (1999) argued that new media, such as instant messaging and online communication, are limited in conveying the same amount of information as a face-to-face conversation. Specifically, when two communicators are not in the same place, physical contact and other nonverbal cues such as olfactory cues become impossible (Kock, 2004). Henderson and Gilding (2004) illustrated that communicating via lean mediums could affect the effectiveness and amount of self-disclosure, thereby influencing reciprocity and trust. While this study was conducted within an interpersonal context, these findings suggest organizational implications. Sheer's (2011) study discovered that a popular reason for the abundance of instant message use between friends is the ability to control information and self-presentation, which could also be applied to co-worker relationships. Additionally, D'Urso and Rains (2008) found support indicating that richness is based on perception and that richness may be shaped by interpersonal factors, such as one's relevant experiences, which is another finding that may lend insight into communication channel satisfaction between co-workers.

As new technologies increasingly become integrated into organizations, the channels of communication available to employees continue to expand. Media channels vary greatly in their richness (Lengel & Daft, 1988). Flyers and bulletins are considered the leanest form of communication, as these are limited in their ability to transmit multiple cues and typically contain fewer cues than richer mediums (Lengel & Daft, 1988). Conversely, face-to-face communication is considered the richest medium because it can transmit multiple cues and information at once (Lengel & Daft, 1988). Richness of the channel is dependent upon the ability to communicate information, the ability to handle multiple cues, feedback rate, and the amount of personal focus (Lengel & Daft, 1988). These factors may also be the reason why some channels would be more appealing to teleworkers of differing personality types such as email, instant messaging, and video communication.

Channel Expansion Theory

Channel expansion theory was conceptualized in an attempt to reconcile previous media richness research (Carlson & Zmud, 1999). While media richness theory has generally been supported when tested on traditional media such as face-to-face and phone communication, the findings have been inconsistent about new media such as e-mail (Lengel & Daft, 1988). Thus, the central premise of channel expansion theory is that an individual's experiences are important factors influencing a person's perception of channel richness. Channel expansion theory argues that each person develops a richness perception for communication channels, specifically influenced by four experiences: experience with the channel, experience with the messaging topic, experience with the organizational context, and experience with communication co-participants (Carlson & Zmud, 1999). Increases in these four types of experience should allow people to articulate and recognize indicators that signal rapid feedback, multiple cues, natural language, and personal focus. For example, co-workers who frequently communicate via email will become more aware of how to convey different levels of formality and communicate subtleties with more experience. Therefore, these types of experiences are positively related to a person's perception of a channel's richness (Carlson & Zmud, 1999).

Similar to how people develop experience with a channel, they also develop experience with communication partners, such as co-workers and supervisors. As people communicate with a specific communication partner, they begin to develop a knowledge base for that person, allowing them to communicate messages tailored to their partner making for a richer communication experience. This can be accomplished through using cues relevant to him or her, referring to shared experience, or using common language (Carlson & Zmud, 1999). This type of knowledge is acquired through on-going communication and the use of one or more knowledge-generating strategies to develop knowledge about others (Walther, 1996). Additionally, as people develop experience with a communication topic, they develop a knowledge base for the topic, allowing for richer communication experiences (Carlson & Zmud, 1999). When communication partners have similar topic experience, richer messages can be facilitated through leveraging shared understanding. As such, communication partners can interpret messages received about a topic more or less richly based on their topic knowledge (Carlson & Zmud, 1999). Finally, people develop a knowledge base centered upon the organizational context in which they are communicating. This allows for communication partners to encode messages with shared symbols and/or organizational cultural references for a richer communication experience, although this idea has found only partial support in empirical research (Carlson & Zmud, 1999).

While experience with communication partners, knowledge, and organizational context are essential to perceptions of media richness, these concepts alone do not fully explain channel perceptions. The social influence model of technology use refers to individual beliefs concerning the appropriate use of a channel as well as perceptions of a channel's richness and demonstrates that these perceptions are in part socially constructed and therefore subject to social influence (Carlson & Zmud, 1999). Research about the social influence model has engendered mixed results. For example, in Carlson and Zmud's two-wave study, support was only found in one group. Although rationalized as a research design error, this was not the first study to find a lack of support for the social influence model (Schmitz & Fulk, 1991). However, D'Urso and Rains' (2008) study did find that perceptions of media richness are socially constructed, which is in line with the social influence model.

9.1.2 Communication Satisfaction and Generational Differences: Our Data

Downs and Hazen's (1977) *Communication Satisfaction Scale* was implemented to index the degree of satisfaction with communication within one's organization. This scale contains five subdimensions, including: personal feedback, organizational identification, communication climate, horizontal communication, and relationship with supervisor. Overall means for the main scale and all subscales were densely concentrated above the midpoint, ranging from 3.97 (relationship with supervisor) to 3.61 (communication climate). Differences across generations are presented below in Table 9.1.

Table 9.1 Generational Differences in the Communication Satisfaction Scale and Subscales

Measure	Baby Boomers M(SD)	Gen X M(SD)	Millennials M(SD)	F (2, 1147)	eta^2
Communication Satisfaction	3.94(.76)	3.77(.86)	3.76(.81)	1.989	.00
Personal Feedback	3.82(1.00)	3.62(1.07)	3.64(.99)	1.358	.00
Organizational Integration	**4.12(.80)**[a]	3.89(.94)[a,b]	**3.81(.88)**[b]	5.575*	.01
Communication Climate	3.72(.99)	3.55(1.03)	3.61(1.00)	.963	.00
Horizontal Communication	3.86(.73)	3.81(.78)	3.83(.77)	.148	.00
Relationship with Supervisor	**4.19(.91)**[a]	3.96(1.03)[a,b]	**3.93(.96)**[b]	3.049*	.01

**p < .001, *p < .05.
[a,b]Significant differences between groups as determined by Tukey HSD post hocs. Scores which significantly differ from the other two scores are bolded.

The results of the between-groups comparisons below reveal minor differences between some generational groups on two of the subscales. Overall, the results show a high degree of communication satisfaction. Two subscales see Baby Boomers reporting significantly greater satisfaction in: *organizational integration*, which is concerned with the degree to which employees receive information that is pertinent to their immediate responsibilities, and greater satisfactions with their relationship with their supervisors. Baby Boomers differ only from Millennials on these two scales, as Gen X falls squarely in between each group and does not differ from either.

This is a particularly useful scale to measure communication satisfaction because it examines the different dimensions that work together to create communication satisfaction. It is not surprising that Baby Boomers are higher on organizational integration. This could be explained through another factor, such as length of time employed by the organization. Even if that did not explain this finding, overall level of work experience could. Since Baby Boomers have been a part of the workforce for a longer period of time than other generations in this study, they have likely learned how to integrate faster and evaluate their integration differently than they did earlier in their career. Conversely, this could help to explain why there is a stagnation among Gen X. Early in their careers, they probably experienced a "honeymoon" phase of employment when they were learning and happy to be employed and soaking everything in, trying to understand how they would evaluate workplace communication. Then, as their experience grew, their perceptions changed because they had baseline knowledge, which could cause their perceptions of communication satisfaction, in this instance, to drop or plateau. This is likely why our findings show Gen X to be lower on some dimensions.

9.2 Generational Perspectives on Job Satisfaction

Job satisfaction refers to how content an individual is with his or her job (West & Berman, 2009). Job satisfaction can also be defined as an affective relationship to one's job that is a function of situational factors, including nature of the work, human resources elements, and the organizational environment (Boswell, Shipp, Payne, & Culbertson, 2009). Previous research about job satisfaction and age remains inconclusive. Therefore, it is unclear if there is a link between job satisfaction and generational membership.

One of the biggest reasons why there is inconsistency in research about age and job satisfaction is because job satisfaction remains stable over time for many employees. However, older employees tend to either maintain their level of job satisfaction over time or experience a decrease in job satisfaction because the number of opportunities available to them decreases (Applebaum, Serena, & Shapiro, 2005). In a study of hospitality workers, generational differences between Millennials and Baby Boomers were found to have significant moderating effects on the relationship between emotional exhaustion and job satisfaction and turnover intention (Lu & Gursoy, 2013). In a comprehensive study conducted by the Society for Human Resource Management, (SHRM, 2014), it was reported that most Millennials are satisfied with their job and that compensation and job security are the two main contributors to their evaluation and feelings of job satisfaction. They also feel satisfied with their job when they are motivated by their work goals, which encourages leaders to help Millennial employees set goals related to their job. Members of Gen X, however, tend to report the lowest levels of job satisfaction because they feel like they are not rewarded enough for their hard work and dedication to their organizations (MetLife, 2019).

9.2.1 Previous Research and Theory

As previously mentioned earlier in this chapter, job satisfaction is a multidimensional construct that is influenced by several other factors, including, but not limited to: organizational culture, communication, leadership, personality, and teleworking. This section will briefly outline some of the previous research findings related to job satisfaction, with the note that this is not an exhaustive overview of this multidimensional construct that is a robust area of research.

An early model of job satisfaction research proposed the two-factor model (Herzberg, Maunser, & Snyderman, 1959), which later gave way to the global approach for understanding job satisfaction. The global approach studies separate job parts that are likely to promote or prevent an individual's level of job satisfaction (Sowmya & Panchanatham, 2011). This informed another model of job satisfaction by Hackman and Oldman (1975), which considered five variables to create "motivating potential," which is the degree to which an employee's motivation can be influenced. Over time, researchers turned to more cognitive conceptualizations of job satisfaction, which is where the field remains today, examining variables that include the employee's needs and how they perceive job satisfaction.

Through cognitive research, we have learned job satisfaction is dependent on many things beyond an employee's frame of mind and also influenced by organizational factors like culture, size, salary, and working conditions or environment. For example, there is a large body of work that examines the job satisfaction of teleworking employees, which has become a renewed interest due to the pandemic that occurred in 2020 and forced organizations to allow many employees to work remotely.

A study conducted in 2005 found a curvilinear relationship between teleworking and job satisfaction, arguing that at a certain point, teleworking leads to less employee satisfaction (Golden, Veiga, & Simsek, 2006). Specifically, Golden and Viega argued that in small amounts, teleworkers are more satisfied because they experience all the benefits of teleworking, while minimizing the disadvantages of teleworking, such as isolation and lack of interpersonal workplace relationships. However, when employees telework regularly, or exclusively, they may start to experience the disadvantages more heavily than the advantages, and therefore have less job satisfaction. Teleworking initially, and in smaller amounts, increases job satisfaction due to its many benefits. Conversely, as the level of teleworking increases and becomes more frequent or exclusive, job satisfaction decreases and at some point, plateaus. These results show that teleworking is complex, and job satisfaction can vary for a number of different reasons, such as the amount of time-spent teleworking (Golden et al., 2006).

In contrast to the study conducted by Golden et al. (2006), a meta-analysis suggested a positive relationship between teleworking and job satisfaction (Gajendran & Harrison, 2007) by demonstrating positive direct effects between teleworking and job satisfaction, mostly attributed to the many benefits teleworking provides employees. In fact, in contrast to previous findings, the meta-analysis did not find any negative effects of teleworking on workplace social ties. Indeed, the meta-analysis revealed that while there are disadvantages to teleworking, the advantages and benefits of teleworking outweigh the disadvantages when it comes to job satisfaction but did not account for the possibility communication channel satisfaction may play in the teleworking and job satisfaction relationship. Finally, Smith, Patmos, and Pitts (2018) found that personality composition does affect the relationship between teleworking and job satisfaction; for example, those who are higher in extraversion, openness, agreeableness, and conscientiousness are best suited for job satisfaction in teleworking environments.

Another major area of inquiry is the relationship between job satisfaction and leadership. Unsurprisingly, employees are more satisfied in organizations that are flexible and that emphasize communication and reward employees (McKinnon, Harrison, Chow, & Wu, 2003), which is greatly influenced by leadership style. Within job satisfaction research, two types of leadership have been studied: transactional leadership and transformational leadership. Transactional leaders act within existing organizational culture, wheres transformational leaders initiate change and can adapt the organizational culture to their own values (Belias & Koustelios, 2014). When leadership style is a match to the employee's values and vision, job satisfaction is positively influenced (Chang & Lee, 2007). Other research has supported the idea that transformational leadership can lead to greater job satisfaction (Bushra, Usman, & Naveed, 2011; Emery & Barker, 2007; Riaz, Akram, & Ijaz, 2011).

9.2.2 Job Satisfaction and Generational Differences: Our Data

Job Satisfaction was measured with a six-item, unidimensional scale from Pond and Geyer (1991). The scale demonstrated excellent reliability, Cronbach's alpha = .966. Greater scores on this measure indicate greater satisfaction.

Although the mean score on Job Satisfaction for Baby Boomers ($M = 3.96$, $SD = 1.09$) was slightly higher than both Gen X ($M = 3.71$, $SD = 1.81$) and Millennials ($M = 3.75$, $SD = 1.02$), that difference failed to reach statistical significance ($F(2, 1147) = 1.957$, $p = .142$, partial eta squared = .00). This pattern of findings, where Baby Boomers' raw scores on job satisfaction are higher, but not significantly so, is similar to the findings reported for Communication Satisfaction above. The results presented in this chapter note a couple of areas where Baby Boomers are slightly more satisfied with communication in their organizations, but no significant differences emerged in overall communication satisfaction of job satisfaction across the three generations explored here.

For similar reasons, it is not surprising that there are not statistically significant generational differences within job satisfaction. Knowing that job satisfaction is a multidimensional construct, this information can be used to help inform future research to better determine, where, if at all, generational differences might influence job satisfaction. Our findings also demonstrate that there is a lot of room to further improve job satisfaction and make it even stronger, through initiatives that enhance or maintain workplace communication.

9.3 Best Practices for Creating a Satisfying Workplace

This chapter has demonstrated the interrelatedness of communication satisfaction and job satisfaction with several other workplace variables including organizational culture, support, leadership, and individual differences. Therefore, the best practices for creating a satisfying workplace among multigenerational employees reflects the relationship that these constructs have with others.

Best Practice 1: Consider Culture

As previous research indicates, organizational culture is really central to understanding satisfaction. If issues exist with constant miscommunications or high levels of communication dissatisfaction, there is most likely a cultural block somewhere within the organization. Similarly, if the retention rate of employees is low, morale is low, and you know that a lot of employees are dissatisfied for a prolonged period of time, you need to look to the organizational culture to address the problem and make changes that promote a culture of satisfaction. This is best measured by looking at employee satisfaction surveys and analyzing exit interview data to understand why people are leaving and if there is any opportunity to make changes that can increase retention and overall satisfaction. The fact is, satisfied employees stay with organizations, so turnover rate is a key metric for understanding employee satisfaction.

Best Practice 2: Communication is Central

The information within this chapter also demonstrated the central role of communication. Although culture is vital to understanding satisfaction, culture is only shared through various forms of communication. When communication is poor throughout an organization, job satisfaction will likely be lower. Conversely, when communication is satisfying and employees feel heard, informed, and able to easily share information, they are likely to report greater levels of both communication and job satisfaction. Refer back to the information in Chapter 7 about supportive communication to improve employee communication satisfaction, which does not seem to have statistically significant generational differences.

Best Practice 3: Technology is a Tool

Technology has overtaken communication and the workplace. Previous research does indicate that there are generational differences related to technology in the workplace, and this is an important consideration with regard to communication and job satisfaction. Generational differences may be present among teleworkers when it comes to job satisfaction.

Consistently using inappropriate channels to share information can lead to lower levels of communication satisfaction, which over time can have a negative and cumulative effect on job satisfaction. Therefore, organizations need to be mindful about the use of technology and not only create policies that promote healthy and satisfactory use but also encourage leaders to model this behavior accordingly to better demonstrate and build satisfaction levels among a multigenerational workforce.

9.4 Conclusion

Communication satisfaction and job satisfaction are highly correlated for every workforce, not just a multigenerational one. Therefore, it is important to understand the different variables that can positively and negatively impact both, which can be influenced by generational membership. The findings from our study are descriptive and demonstrate that when satisfaction is present, there are negligible if any, generational differences among employees. Therefore, this should be encouraging news for organizations and leaders to promote effective communication in the workplace for long-term job satisfaction.

References

Akkirman, A. D., & Harris, D. L. (2005). Organizational communication satisfaction in the virtual workplace. *Journal of Management Development*, *24*, 397–409.

Applebaum, S., Serena, M., & Shapiro, B. (2005). Generation "X" and the Boomers: An analysis of realities and myths. *Management Research News*, *28*, 1–32.

Belias, D., & Koustelios, A. (2014). Organizational culture and job satisfaction: A review. *International Review of Management and Marketing*, *4*, 132–149.

Boswell, W., Shipp, A., Payne, S., & Culbertson, S. (2009) Changes in newcomer job satisfaction over time: Examining the pattern of honeymoon and hangovers. *Journal of Applied Psychology*, *94*, 844–858.

Bushra, F., Usman, A., & Naveed, A. (2011). Effect of transformational leadership on employee's job satisfaction and organizational commitment in banking sector of Lahore (Pakistan). *International Journal of Business and Social Science*, *2*, 261–267.

Carlson, J., & Zmud, R. (1999). Channel expansion theory and the experiential nature of media richness perceptions. *Academy of Management Journal*, *42*, 153–170.

Chang, S., & Lee, M. (2007). A study on relationship among leadership, organizational culture, the operation of learning organization and employee's job satisfaction. *The Learning Organization*, *14*, 155–185.

Crino, M. D., & White, M. C. (1981). Satisfaction in communication: An examination of the Downs-Hazen measure. *Psychological Reports, 49,* 831–838.

Downs, C. W., & Hazen, M. D. (1977). A factor analytic study of communication satisfaction. *Journal of Business Communication, 14,* 63–73.

D'Urso, S., & Rains, S. (2008). Examining the scope of channel expansion: A test of channel expansion theory with new and traditional communication media. *Management Communication Quarterly, 21,* 486–507.

Easton, S., & Bommelje, R. (2011). Interpersonal communication consequences of email non-response. *Florida Communication Journal, 39,* 45–63.

Emery, C., & Barker, K. (2007). The effect of transactional and transformational leadership styles on the organizational commitment and job satisfaction of customer contact personnel. *Journal of Organizational Culture, Communications, and Conflict, 11,* 77–90.

Gajendran, R., & Harrison, D. (2007). The good, the bad, and the unknown about telecommuting: Meta-analysis of psychological mediators and individual consequences. *Journal of Applied Psychology, 92,* 1524–1541.

Golden, T., Veiga, J., & Simsek, Z. (2006). Telecommuting's differential impact on work-family conflict: Is there no place like home? *Journal of Applied Psychology, 91,* 1340–1350.

Green, M., Hilken, J., Friedman, H., Grossman, K., Gasiewski, J., & Adler, R. (2005). Communication via instant messenger: Short and long-term effects. *Journal of Applied Social Psychology, 35,* 445–462.

Hackman, J., & Oldman, G. (1975). Development of the Job Diagnostic Survey. *Journal of Applied Psychology, 60,* 159–170.

Henderson, S., & Gilding, M. (2004). "I've never clicked this much with anyone in my life": Trust and hyper-personal communication in online friendships. *New Media & Society, 6,* 487–506.

Herzberg, F., Maunser, B., & Snyderman, B. (1959). *The motivation to work.* John Wiley & Sons, Inc.

Hollingshead, A., McGrath, J., & O'Connor, K. (1993). Group task performance and communication technology: A longitudinal study of computer-mediated versus face-to-face work groups. *Small Group Research, 24,* 307–333.

Jacobsen, D. (1999). Impression formation in cyberspace: Online expectations and offline experiences in text-based virtual communities. *Journal of Computer-Mediated Communication, 5.* doi: 10.1111=j.1083–6101.1999.tb00333.x

Kock, N. (2004). The psychobiological model: Towards a new theory of computer-mediated communication based on Darwinian evolution. *Organizational Science, 15,* 327–349.

Kurland, N., & Bailey, D. E. (1999). Telework: The advantages and challenges of working here, there, anywhere, and anytime. *Organizational Dynamics, 28,* 53–68.

Lengel, R., & Daft, R. (1988). The selection of communication media as an executive skill. *The Academy of Management Executive, 2,* 225–232.

Lu, A., & Gursoy, D. (2013). Impact of job burnout on satisfaction and turnover intention: Do generational differences matter? *Hospitality & Tourism Research, 40,* 210–235.

McKinnon, L., Harrison, L., Chow, W., & Wu, A. (2003). Organizational culture: Association with commitment, job satisfaction, propensity to remain and information sharing in Taiwan. *International Journal of Business Studies, 11,* 25–44.

MetLife (2019). Thriving in the new work-life world. MetLife's 17th annual U.S. employee benefit trends study. https://www.metlife.com/content/dam/metlifecom/us/ebts/pdf/MetLife-Employee-Benefit-Trends-Study-2019.pdf

Park., H. S., & Raile, A. N. W. (2010). Perspective taking and communication satisfaction in coworker dyads. *Journal of Business Psychology, 25,* 569–581.

Pincus, J. D. (1986). Communication satisfaction, job satisfaction, and job performance. *Human Communication Research, 12,* 395–419.

Pond, S., & Geyer, P. (1991). Differences in the relation between job satisfaction and perceived work alternatives among older and younger blue-collar workers. *Journal of Vocational Behavior, 39,* 251–262.

Riaz, T., Akram, M., & Ijaz, H. (2011). Impact of transformational leadership style on affective employees commitment: An empirical study of banking sector in Islamabad (Pakistan). *The Journal of Commerce, 3,* 43–51.

Schmitz, J., & Fulk, J. (1991). Organizational colleagues, media richness, and electronic mail: A test of the social influence model of technology use. *Communication Research, 18,* 487–523.

Sheer, V. (2011). Teenagers' use of MSN features, discussion topics, and online friendship development: The impact of media richness and communication control. *Communication Quarterly, 59,* 82–103.

Sheer, V., & Chen, L. (2004). Improving media richness theory. *Management Communication Quarterly, 18,* 76–93.

SHRM (2014). Millennial employees' job satisfaction and engagement. *SHRM Research Spotlight.* Retrieved from: https://www.shrm.org/hr-today/trends-and-forecasting/research-and-surveys/Documents/Millennials-Job-Satisfaction-Engagement-Flyer.pdf

Sias, P. M., Pedersen, H., Gallagher, E. B., & Kopaneva, I. (2012). Workplace friendship in the electronically connected organization. *Human Communication Research, 38,* 253–279.

Smith, S. A., Patmos, A. K., & Pitts, M. J. (2018). Communication and teleworking: A study of communication channel satisfaction, personality, and job satisfaction for teleworking employees. *International Journal of Business Communication, 55,* 44–68. doi: 10.1177/2329488415589101

Sowmya, K., & Panchanatham, N. (2011). Factors influencing job satisfaction of banking sector employees in Chennai, India. *Journal of Law and Conflict Resolution, 3,* 76–79.

Tsai, M., & Chuang, S. (2009). An integrated process model of communication satisfaction and organizational outcomes. *Social Behavior and Personality, 37,* 825–834.

Walther, J. (1996). Computer-mediated communication: Impersonal, inter-personal and hyperpersonal interaction. *Communication Research, 23*, 3–43.
Watson-Manheim, M. B., & Belanger, F. (2007). Media repertoires: Dealing with the multiplicity of media choices. *MIS Quarterly, 31*, 267–293.
West, J., & Berman, E. (2009). Job satisfaction of public managers in special districts. *Review of Public Personnel Administration, 29*, 327–353.

10 Remote and Virtual Work

This chapter describes the changing nature of the workplace specifically focusing on remote and virtual work. The evolving nature of work, especially surrounding digital expectations, will be discussed.

10.1 The Evolving Nature of Work

At the time of this writing, the very nature of work has changed dramatically on an international scale. On December 31st, 2019, China confirmed an unknown cause for a handful of pneumonia cases. By the first week of January 2020, this unknown disease had been labeled as a new strain of coronavirus effectively named COVID-19. Travel bans, economic declines, event cancellations, lockdowns, and stay-at-home orders ensued as the virus spread worldwide and the death toll rose.

In essence, this new coronavirus strand impacted everything, especially work. From an economic standpoint, COVID-19 created unprecedented "modern-era" job loss. In April 2020, unemployment in the United States reached upward of 14%, or around 23 million unemployed workers. Some workers were furloughed with subsequent layoffs days, weeks, or months after. Not all jobs lost could have been performed in a remote capacity; however, many jobs were saved because of a virtual transition.

Though the COVID-19 pandemic of 2020 ushered forth a new era wherein remote and virtual work became more prominent, remote and virtual work are not new phenomena. Even as early as 1989, Peter Drucker supposedly determined that working from the office was obsolete (Streitfield, 2020). Mokhtarian (1991) defined telecommuting, broadly, as the use of "telecommunications technology to partially or completely replace the commute to and from work" (p. 1). This distinction, developed by Mokhtarian 30 years ago, has only somewhat changed. Remote work today still encompasses a work-from-somewhere-else mantra, but the National Institute of Health (NIH) does distinguish remote work from telework among their own workers. According to National Institutes of Health (2020), remote work constitutes a permanent designation in which the employee works permanently from an alternative worksite, while telework is regular or ad hoc but does require the employee to report to the office at times. These distinctions are helpful for considering next steps in terms of defining the structure of work for employees. Semantics, especially now, are crucial as organizations determine how to proceed for telecommuting or remote workers. No matter how those distinctions are communicated organizationally, the overall sentiment remains the same: work not consistently conducted in the physical office setting.

There are, generally, different types of remote work and subsequently different remote workers. Nickson and Siddons (2012) identify a home worker as anyone who is based at home and who uses their home as their main office space for at least two days a week. Home office working, though, is different from coworking, where individuals still work at a physical office location but work alongside other unaffiliated professionals (Spinuzzi, 2012). Coworking, post pandemic, has become less popular, and the term "remote work" generally applies to a virtual context. With that said, a more helpful all-encompassing term was coined by Grant, Wallace, and Spurgeon (2013) who refer to remote e-working as work completed anywhere and at any time. This reality, that work can legitimately be accomplished anywhere regardless of location, presents incredible opportunities and challenges for organizations today.

Workers in remote contexts experience a different work environment from the traditional face-to-face worker. For one, they have limited face-to-face interaction with their peers or supervisors (Charalampous, Grant, Tramontano, & Michailidis, 2019) which can have negative effects on support and employee engagement. In addition, the actual environment where remote workers conduct their business can lead to home conflict and distraction (Eddleston and Mulki, 2017). These issues create potential difficulty for remote workers, but these challenges can be overcome.

The modern workplace, highlighted by shifts in remote and virtual work, has changed in other ways as well. The delivery of work, or how we conduct our work and in what context, is not the only issue to consider. The actual work done has also become a topic of discussion. The virtual work revolution has provided an opportunity for work "gigification" (Veen, Kaine, Goods, & Barratt, 2020). This means, basically, that new services and novel solutions to niche problems have been answered through many different platforms or opportunities. Generally, "gig" work is driven by customer demand

and the individual worker, typically, has what is needed to perform the work. Usually "gig" work is paid at a piece rate (think freelance), and there is usually an intermediary platform that connects client and worker. The ability to not just work for a full-time employer but also conduct business virtual for "gig" platforms has placed a premium on remote and virtual work contexts.

This evolution of work makes leadership all the more important. Flood (2019) believes, and rightly so, that leading a remote or virtual workforce requires formal policies, additional resources, and innovative operations for individuals to share ideas and achieve objectives. Thus, performance management, relationship building, communication, and training all become even more important in a virtual or remote context (Hickman & Pendall, 2018). As remote work continues to become more popular in a "post-pandemic" world, leaders need to be adept not only at managing generational differences but also doing so in potentially remote and virtual environments.

10.2 Work Post-Pandemic

Since the pandemic, an unprecedented number of employers have begun working from home. In July 2020, job losses that occurred as a result of the COVID-19 pandemic were up to three times as large for non-remote workers (Angelucci, Angrisani, Bennett, Kapteyn, & Schaner, 2020). Not surprisingly, income losses and health challenges were greater during this time for non-remote workers. In addition, similar to the changes wrought by the gig-economy, the actual work conducted in a post-pandemic world varies. Bartik, Cullen, Glaeser, Luca, and Stanton (2020) report that remote work levels are higher post-pandemic but that there are significant variations across industries and that remote work is more common in industries with workers who are better educated and have better pay.

The final verdict on the actual effect and impact of remote work continues to be a matter of debate. Some, like Ozimek (2020), suggest that the remote work experiment has done better than expected. However, as will be discussed later, other dimensions related to productivity have yet to come to true fruition (Chebly, Schiano, & Mehra, 2020). Almost certainly, organizations will continue to figure out how to increase effectiveness and productivity in the remote workplace. However, as organizations strive to create environments that are flexible and adaptable for a new generation of employees, the underlying necessity to make operations, policies, and procedures remote friendly continues to confront remote leaders and workers.

10.3 Remote Work and Virtual Effectiveness

In a time that now seems like ages ago, Marissa Mayer, then CEO of Yahoo, banned remote work (Calvo, 2013). Mayer's decision was nothing short of controversial; today it would seem outrageous. Even before Millennials infiltrated the workplace, the concept of remote work and the ability to finish tasks virtually was debated but did find friendly audiences in several different industries. As Millennials became more ingratiated in the workplace, the demands for remote and virtual opportunities increased (Calvo, 2013). This reality has become even more prominent in our post-pandemic world. However, it is important to consider the benefits as well as the challenges of working in a remote or virtual context.

Benefits of Remote Work

It is important to note, first, that remote work can be successful because of great technological connectivity (Messenger & Gschwind, 2016). Without new technological advances, remote work would cease to exist, much less serve as a tangible alternative to face-to-face office work. New remote work tools and platforms are discussed later in the chapter, but before having a philosophical discussion about the merits of virtual work, it is important to note that as the technology goes, so goes the ability to do what employees need to do outside of the office.

The benefits of remote work are multifaceted and help more than just the individual employee. For one, remote work can decrease costs associated with purchasing a physical office or work location as well as maintaining that physical space (Felstead & Henseke, 2017). This reality helps affirm at least one potential organizational benefit. The necessary physical resources diminish as employees spend more time working from a non-office location. Kylili et al. (2020) go further and state that the lack of commute and necessity to be in a physical location also positively impacts the environment. For instance, decreased commuting leads to fewer emissions and a reduced carbon footprint. Additional environmental benefits include reduced noise pollution, reduced need for roads and infrastructure, and reduced road congestion (Kylili et al., 2020).

The concept of work-from-home, or today's even more appropriate mantra of work-from-anywhere (Choudhury, Foroughi, & Larson, 2020), offer employees great flexibility. This flexibility, however, must be managed appropriately. Staples, Hulland, and Higgins (1999) noted increased perceptions of employee productivity when their self-efficacy and perceptions of remote work effectiveness are high. This is important to note. Employees may not naturally find themselves astute at remote work operations, especially if the concept or experience is new, but organizations can employ training mechanisms to help employees understand expectations. Interestingly, Baker, Avery, and Crawford (2007) found that organizational and job-related factors are more likely to affect the satisfaction of work from home or work from anywhere employees. Meaning, it is less about household characteristics and work styles and still, like traditional face-to-face work contexts, more about the job and the culture itself.

Continually, increasing work life balance is a strong argument for remote work offerings. A better or more balanced work life environment can certainly be achieved if people work from home (Kerslake, 2002). The time saved by forgoing a commute and potentially saving on childcare are extremely beneficial. Yet, working virtually does present opportunities for overwork.

Potential Challenges of Remote Work

The concept of overwork, or the inability of employees to separate work from life on an even more extreme basis, is one of the most pressing questions, and challenges, of remote work. While work life balance in some ways is enhanced through remote and virtual work, the ability for employees to work too much is a real concern (Grant et al., 2013). Working from home does create challenges as employees try to separate their work from their regular life without clear differentiating boundaries.

In addition, the actual office environment, and the lack of social relationships at work can be problematic. Workers have said they miss office interactions and have a sense and feeling of isolation (Grant et al., 2013; Mann & Holdsworth, 2003). This isolation, which can be overcome, somewhat, with real-time, synchronous video or phone calls, is still a real manifestation of a potentially lonely situation.

Virtual team collaboration, creativity, and overall productivity may also suffer. Eisenberg and Krishnan (2018) identify five virtual team challenges, including trust and relationships, communication and knowledge sharing, perceptions and decision making, leadership, and diversity. These five challenges do not occur solely in a virtual context, but it is still worth noting that they can potentially become more pressing when workers are only interacting and communicating through remote platforms.

Finally, human resources professionals note issues related to overall employee clarity. For one, a general lack of policies and procedures are in place (Flood, 2019) across the spectrum as organizations try to identify the best ways to engage virtual workers while holding them accountable. The problems with work life balance and the ability to work at all times throughout the day prove especially problematic for hourly workers, who, in many instances, cannot go over a certain time threshold without incurring required overtime pay. These challenges are not insurmountable but certainly should cause organizations to consider best practices for engaging and managing remote employees.

10.4　Remote Work Tools and Platforms

The platforms used to perform remote work continue to provide new avenues for increased productivity; however, that was not always the case. The 1970s brought to the forefront an explosion of personal computers and, eventually, work-from-home monitoring software. The tool itself, the personal computer, was somewhat nullified without the ability for organizations to hold employees accountable through systemic network software. The trend continued with the advent of the Internet and the incredible capabilities the world wide web afforded. In the 1990s, the invention of WIFI provided greater geographic flexibility as workers could forsake their hard-wired Internet connections. After these foundational developments, specifically network and tools, the creation of monitoring software and actual remote work platforms started to increase. Eventually, with the creation of the smartphone, all roads converged into uber remote convenience.

From a policy standpoint, several governmental actions in the United States popularized or helped normalize remote work. For one, in 1995, Congress approved permanent funding for "flexiplace" work-related equipment for federal employees. Then in 2000, the DOT Appropriations Act was enacted. This law required all executive agencies to develop telecommuting policies. Five years later, in 2005, President Barack Obama signed the Telework Enhancement Act requiring federal agencies to create policies for employees to work remotely. As these policies were enacted, the actual number of remote workers and remote platform users continued to grow.

In 1987, 1.5 million documented telecommuters worked across the USA. Before the pandemic of 2020, 7 million people reported working remotely in the United States, roughly 3.5% of the population. In 2016, the team collaboration tool, Slack, had 4 million active daily users and 9 million by 2019. By 2018, 70% of the world's population reported working

Table 10.1 Remote Work Tools, Use, and General Purpose

Remote Work Tool	General Use	Purpose
Slack	Team communication application	Get instant feedback and connect with colleagues
Zoom	Video conferencing application	"Zoom calls" allow employees to meet synchronously over video
Trello	Project management software	Uses visual cues and aesthetic design to increase remote group productivity
Google Drive	File management application	Digital file management tool that allows for synchronous collaboration and file storage
Zapier	Workflow automation	Zapier allows applications to connect somewhat seamlessly to allow greater functionality and moves data between different applications

remotely at least once a week. By 2019, the team video collaboration tool, Zoom, reported more than 50,000 customers that had more than 10 employees. In 2017, Zoom reported more than 700,000 users. These platforms continue to grow in popularity and overall efficiency.

The market today is flooded with remote work platform options. For simplicity, we developed a table to summarize different remote work platforms. The list below is not exhaustive and mentions tools primarily popular in 2020 but does provide a glimpse into the varying types of workflow platforms and their focus (Table 10.1).

The list above does not account for duplicate products, like Skype or previous Google Hangouts for video conferencing, all-in-one platforms like Microsoft Teams, or even additional tools like Serene, Toggl, Spark, or remote desktop that allow for even more creativity and efficiency. These tools all can be helpful, but employers would be wise to think strategically about communication in their remote work environment and approach these tools with intentionality and purpose. Just because a tool exists does not mean it is best for every business or organization.

10.5 Generational Differences and Remote Work

As remote work becomes more popular, and remote work tools become more widespread, a look at how employees feel about remote and virtual work can provide organizational clarity. While not the only framework to consider employee perceptions of remote work, generational differences can help supervisors and executives determine how their employees differ in their remote work perceptions. With that said, the overall differences may not be as distinct as one would assume, especially in a world overrun with remote workers and remote work opportunities.

Before considering legitimate generational differences in this regard, it is worth noting again what different generations value. Millennials, for instance, are tech-savvy and appreciate collaborative work, Gen Xers tend to rank lower on executive presence, and Baby Boomers are notably loyal to their organizations but may not adapt quickly. In addition, like Millennials, Gen Xers appreciate flexibility and want to be independent workers. Zimmerman (2016) reports that Millennials appreciate working from home, but an even greater number of Boomer and Gen X employees prefer a work from home option. Millennials are generally used to the always-available workplace, yet they continually rank work-life balance and work flexibility as highly-rated work rewards.

Kennelly (2015) correctly identifies that new employee character-istics are shifting in terms of when people work, how people share jobs, and how individuals are evaluated on their performance. However, even as these shifts occur, employees generally desire some sort of flexibility in terms of how their job is performed (Rousseau, 2015). This trend is probably not going away.

Recognizing that all generations prefer flexibility, in some capacity, all workers may not be prime candidates for work-from-home or work-from-anywhere options. As organizations continue to explore remote work options, individual employee desires; the actual job description and primary responsibilities; and remote work capacity should all be considered.

10.6 Best Practices

Best Practice 1: Consider the Purpose of Remote Work

While it may be easy – especially in a work world initially ravaged by a pandemic – to assume jobs work best in a remote context, employers and supervisors should consider all facets of the job, the organizational culture, and individual employees before demanding or suggesting employees work from home. Organizations would do well to intentionally explore remote options without assuming individuals should or should not work from home because of personal preferences. This chapter does position remote work as a tangible and realistic option for a host of employees for a number of reasons. As a suggested best practice, though, organizations are encouraged to tread wisely into remote positions.

Best Practice 2: Remote Work Platforms Are NOT Created Equally

While the lists presented above are not exhaustive, they do provide a snippet of the software or platform options available to organizations. However, organizations should navigate platform choices wisely. For one, remember that all software platforms and remote network systems are not created equal. Your organization may not need, for example, all of the features Slack has to offer. Consider your overall internal communication strategy as it relates to remote work platforms. Instead of using all tools available and switching when a new tool arrives on the market, work in a constant state of assessment and analysis, asking how employees use their current software to communicate effectively and what other features are needed in order to conduct appropriate business.

Best Practice 3: Designate Remote Responsibilities as well as Policies and Procedures

The rush to remote work in 2020 highlighted a few issues in the general workplace. For example, when many organizations transitioned to remote work, they were not prepared from a human resources perspective. Specifically, a lack of policies regarding work conducted remotely led to a lack of accountability for both employees and managers in some organizations. Any organization desiring a remote transition should first assess its overall operations and designate what should be completed remotely. After this, designating remote responsibilities for individual employees is crucial. Finally, policies and general procedures for remote work should be clearly communicated to the organization as a whole.

10.7 Conclusion

This chapter presented the current state of remote and virtual work. While remote work may seem relatively new because of the steep increase in remote workers due to global events, the reality is that remote work has existed for decades. This reality should encourage organizations who can move remotely to do so. From a generational perspective, it is interesting to note that employees, generally, across the spectrum appreciate the opportunity to do their work in a flexible environment, remote or otherwise.

This desire transcends generational differences and has become a general desire of employees who believe working from home gives greater work-life balance and offers more flexibility. With that said, organizations should approach remote work wisely. Do not forsake what makes your organizational culture unique in an effort to satisfy the new remote work urge. Instead, take time to think deeply about a potential remote work transition and, where possible, transition slowly and with purpose.

References

Angelucci, M., Angrisani, M., Bennett, D. M., Kapteyn, A., & Schaner, S. G. (2020). *Remote work and the heterogeneous impact of COVID-19 on employment and health* (No. w27749). National Bureau of Economic Research.

Baker, E., Avery, G. C., & Crawford, J. (2007). Satisfaction and perceived productivity when professionals work from home. *Research and Practice in Human Resource Management, 15*, 37–62.

Bartik, A. W., Cullen, Z. B., Glaeser, E. L., Luca, M., & Stanton, C. T. (2020). *What jobs are being done at home during the COVID-19 crisis? Evidence from firm-level surveys* (No. w27422). National Bureau of Economic Research.

Calvo, A. J. (2013). Where's the remote? Facetime, remote work, and implications for performance management. *Cornell HR Review*. http://digitalcommons.ilr.cornell.edu/chrr/45/

Charalampous, M., Grant, C. A., Tramontano, C., & Michailidis, E. (2019). Systematically reviewing remote e-workers' well-being at work: A multidimensional approach. *European Journal of Work and Organizational Psychology, 28*, 51–73.

Chebly, J., Schiano, A., & Mehra, D. (2020). The value of work: Rethinking labor productivity in times of COVID-19 and automation. *American Journal of Economics and Sociology, 79*, 1345–1365. https://doi.org/10.1111/ajes.12357

Choudhury, P., Foroughi, C., & Larson, B. Z. (2020). Work-from-anywhere: The productivity effects of geographic flexibility. In *Academy of Management Proceedings* (Vol. 2020, No. 1, p. 21199). Academy of Management.

Eddleston, K. A., & Mulki, J. (2017). Toward understanding remote workers' management of work–family boundaries: The complexity of workplace embeddedness. *Group & Organization Management, 42*, 346–387.

Eisenberg, J., & Krishnan, A. (2018). Addressing virtual work challenges: learning from the field. *Organization Management Journal, 15*, 78–94.

Felstead, A., & Henseke, G. (2017). Assessing the growth of remote working and its consequences for effort, well-being and work-life balance. *New Technology, Work and Employment, 32*(3), 195–212.

Flood, F. (2019). Leadership in the remote, freelance, and virtual workforce era. In A. Farazmand (Ed.), *Global encyclopedia of public administration, public policy, and governance* (pp. 1–7). Springer. https://doi.org/10.1007/978-3-319-31816-5_3825-1.

Grant, C. A., Wallace, L. M., & Spurgeon, P. C. (2013). An exploration of the psychological factors affecting remote e-worker's job effectiveness, well-being and work-life balance. *Employee Relations, 35*, 527–546.

Hickman, A., & Pendall, R. (2018). The end of the traditional manager. Gallup. https://www.gallup.com/workplace/236108/end-traditional-manager.aspx

Kennelly, J. (2015). Embracing the virtual workforce. *Human Resource Management*, 22–23.

Kerslake, P. (2002). The work/life balance pay-back. *New Zealand Management, 49*, 28–31

Kylili, A., Afxentiou, N., Georgiou, L., Panteli, C., Morsink-Georgalli, P. Z., Panayidou, A., Papouis, C., & Fokaides, P. A. (2020). The role of remote working in smart cities: Lessons learnt from COVID-19 pandemic. *Energy Sources, Part A: Recovery, Utilization, and Environmental Effects, 12*, 1–16.

Mann, S., & Holdsworth, L. (2003). The psychological impact of teleworking: Stress, emotions and health. *New Technology, Work and Employment, 18*, 196–211.

Messenger, J., & Gschwind, L. (2016). Three generations of telework: New ICT and the (R)evolution from home office to virtual office. *New Technology, Work and Employment, 31*, 195–208.

Mokhtarian, P. (1991). Defining telecommuting. *UC Davis: Institute of Transportation Studies*. https://escholarship.org/uc/item/35c4q71r

National Institutes of Health. (2020, November). Remote work. https://hr.nih.gov/working-nih/work-schedules/remote-work

Nickson, D., & Siddons, S. (2012). *Remote working*. Routledge.

Ozimek, A. (2020). The future of remote work. *Available at SSRN 3638597*.

Rousseau, D. (2015). *I-deals: Idiosyncratic deals employees bargain for themselves: Idiosyncratic deals employees bargain for themselves*. Routledge.

Spinuzzi, C. 2012. Working alone together: Coworking as emergent collaborative activity. *Journal of Business and Technical Communication, 26*, 399–441. doi:10.1177/1050651912444070.

Staples, D. S., Hulland, J. S., & Higgins, C. A. (1999). A self-efficacy theory explanation for the management of remote workers in virtual organizations. *Organization Science, 10*, 758–776.

Streitfield, D. (2020, June 29). The long, unhappy history of working from home. *New York Times*. https://www.nytimes.com/2020/06/29/technology/working-from-home-failure.html

Veen, A., Kaine, S., Goods, C., & Barratt, T. (2020). 2 The 'gigification' of work in the 21st century. In *Contemporary work and the future of employment in developed countries* (pp. 15–32). Routledge-Cavendish.

Zimmerman, K. (2016, October 14). Do millennials prefer working from home more than Baby Boomers and Gen X? Forbes. https://www.forbes.com/sites/kaytiezimmerman/2016/10/13/do-millennials-prefer-working-from-home-more-than-baby-boomers-and-gen-x/?sh=475f7eb42070

11 Innovation and Future Challenges

This chapter explores the future of work, including future challenges, expectations, and evolutions. The authors provide information about future generations (i.e. what can we learn from Generation Alpha) and what communication will look like in the workplace of the future.

11.1 The Future of Work

The future of work looks drastically different in a post-pandemic world. However, some innovations we have already implemented, like work-from-anywhere and remote or virtual work, will continue to become more commonplace. Where we conduct our work has been a consistent discussion for years – if not decades – but other realities will distinguish work in a post-2020 world from work environments that came before. This section will preview several new work initiatives that may help define the future of work. Generally, we may see a trend toward what Peters (2017) calls technological unemployment because of so many new technologies replacing traditional vocations.

Automation

As a work phenomenon, automation includes artificial intelligence, autonomous systems, and robotics. Workplace automation replaces or enhances workflow and varying processes through technology. As one could assume, automation offers several benefits, specifically cutting costs and increasing productivity. As a framework or overarching change agent for the modern workplace, automation is in the midst of a renaissance or a revolution. Interestingly, AI and automation experts call our current climate the fourth Industrial Revolution (Sako, 2020). This new revolution brings together artificial intelligence, automation, robotics, genetic engineering, and other technologies. Automation receives mixed reviews from economists and employees as some declare it replaces employment, considering that is what it is designed to do (Autor, 2015). However, Bessen (2019) points out that automation can actually increase opportunities for industry employment. Generally, automation causes employees to, at the very least, learn new skills and new occupations. While opinions vary widely regarding the impact of automation on jobs (Winick, 2018), some clarity waits on the horizon as more companies and industries move to automated processes. In some ways, the COVID-19 pandemic of 2020 forced companies to make decisions about their digital or automated operations. No matter what comes next, automation – and one of the core subsets of automation, artificial intelligence – are certainly a significant category surrounding the future of work and work innovation. From a communication standpoint, the influx of automation brings about several interesting questions related to human capabilities; the need for emotional intelligence and workplace relationships; and the general, overall impact of automation on work and organizational culture.

Artificial Intelligence

The actual definition of artificial intelligence (AI), especially as it relates to a manifestation in the workplace, has been debated, and, unfortunately, no widely accepted definition of artificial intelligence exists. Wang (2019) reiterates the confusion involved with trying to determine one specific AI definition; however, simply, AI includes a "system's ability to correctly interpret external data, to learn from such data, and to use those learnings to achieve specific goals and tasks" (Kaplan & Haenlein, 2019, p. 15). In a work context, AI is predicted to have even more of a holistic globally transformative impact on the economy (Howard, 2019).

AI can be extremely beneficial in the workplace. For one, AI can actually help determine which jobs can be completed by a machine (Sako, 2020). This can significantly increase efficiency and productivity and provides some clarity about what tasks require a human worker for completion. These efficiencies come with some difficulties, and it is incorrect to assume artificial intelligence will just solve all workforce problems. There are some challenges to consider. As AI becomes more popular, additional regulation may be needed (Haenlein & Kaplan, 2019). Humans may need to develop ethics and functional norms surrounding AI (Sako, 2020). Regardless, artificial intelligence will continue to be a significant factor in the future of work.

Inclusive Workplaces

Inclusive work – and diversity and inclusivity as corporate initiatives – have become more popular as organizations wrestle with their hiring procedures and operational biases. Organizations have sought to become more inclusive by creating an atmosphere of psychological safety (Carmeli, Brueller, & Dutton, 2009); establishing transparent hiring practices; and providing equal access to advancement, decision-making, professional development, and other resources (Shore, Cleveland, & Sanchez, 2018). Inclusive workplaces will not occur naturally and instead must be achieved with careful consideration and planning.

Inclusive best practices are numerous. Offerman and Basford (2014) believe that inclusive leaders should work to develop a talent pipeline and that they should confront subtle discrimination. In addition, diversity should be leveraged to increase business performance, and accountability systems and mechanisms should be established (Offerman & Basford, 2014). Employees and other senior leaders should be trained to carry out inclusive efforts. Similarly, Sabharwal (2014) believes inclusive behaviors must be a top down initiative involving fair and equitable treatment of employees so they can influence organizational decisions. As a feature of the modern workplace and an integral part of the future of work, inclusive workplaces and inclusive organizational culture will continue to be an area of consistent study for communication scholars (Rezai, Kolne, Bui, & Lindsay, 2020).

Cloud-Based Collaboration

Cloud-based collaboration and cloud use in general will continue to be a feature of work moving forward. Gallaugher (2014) refers to cloud computing as hardware or software services that occur over the Internet through a third party. Qin, Hsu, and Stern (2016) refer to cloud computing as a form of computation "where the processing and applications mainly reside not on the user's computer or network, but rather on a remote server connected through an Internet connection" (p. 227). The business of cloud computing will continue to grow with an expected revenue of over $240 billion post-2020 (Dignan, 2011).

From a communication standpoint, cloud computing should have far reaching effects, especially on teams, teamwork, and group collaboration. As much of what we do – both as consumers and employees – moves into a cloud-based context, organizations should explore ways to improve collaboration services, specifically by focusing on team strategies surrounding communication, coordination, support, and effort

(Qin, Hsu, & Stern, 2016). As workplaces look to enhance the overall ethos of their organizations, as well as the efficiency of their operations, a thorough look at cloud computing will help increase productivity and overall group learning processes (Hadjileontiadou, Dias, Diniz, & Hadjileontiadis, 2015).

Learning and Development

Though learning and development are not new concepts, they will continue to be important focus areas for corporations and organizations in the future for several reasons. For one, learning and development initiatives continue to be linked to different business performance improvement (Chambel & Sobral, 2011). In addition, different knowledge areas, connected to learning and development, can serve as a key competitive advantage (Drucker, 2000). Generally, the area of learning and development has changed dramatically from one of individual, manual-driven instruction to high-tech interactive and experiential learning (Scurtu, 2015).

As a feature of future work, learning and development is expected to continue to evolve. It is expected that future learning and development will be even more mobile (Bonk, Kim, & Zong, 2005), will be focused not just on knowledge and behavior but also on affect (Barnett, 2012), and will be continually tech-driven and individualized to each learner (Davidson, 2009).

The post-pandemic world will continue to reveal new and necessary learning and development areas. However, it is expected that inclusivity and training in a potentially socially distanced or fully virtual workplace will continue to be a defining feature of learning and development moving forward (McBride, 2020).

Social, Emotional, and Physical Well-being

The other future work foci – automation, artificial intelligence, inclusive workplaces, and learning and development – are related, mostly, to job performance. However, as remote work continues to become more popular, work-life balance and other items related to general employee well-being have become a corporate focus for many organizations. Dodge, Daly, Huyton, and Sanders (2012) define well-being as "the balance point between an individual's resource pool and the challenges faced" (p. 222). Generally, though, well-being in the workplace is defined primarily positive. The fact that the employee is balanced, doing well, and is experiencing more positive emotions than negative emotions in the workplace (Aboobaker, Edward, & Zakkariya, 2019).

The work-from-home and work-from-anywhere culture has brought to the forefront a struggle for many employees, a healthy separation of work-life from home-life. Employees face a challenging context, a complex and blurred boundary between work and life (Hamilton Skurak, Malinen, Naswall, & Kuntz, 2018). In light of these challenges, organizations would do well to focus on programs and initiatives that emphasize employee well-being. As organizations focus on employee well-being, they may see increased productivity and performance (Peiró, Kozusznik, Rodríguez-Molina, & Tordera, 2019.

All told, these future work dynamics are exciting. While uncertainty definitely surrounds some of these developments, our workplaces will adapt. As the workplace of the future continues to evolve, relationships within organizations and initiatives that protect workplace culture should be a continued priority. Workplaces, then, need to appropriately respond not just to changing operations, like automation and artificial intelligence, but also to changing dynamics among employees. We explain how to seamlessly incorporate future generations into the workplace.

11.2 Integrating Future Generations and Creating a Culture of Generational Understanding

This book explores, primarily, relationships among Baby Boomers, Generation Xers, and Millennials. While some of our data and corresponding literature do address members of Generation Z, they are not a core focus of this text. Yet, members of Generation Z, and even those who come after members of Gen Z currently identified as Generation Alpha, should be considered when organizations develop a long-term culture of generational understanding.

Generation Z

Members of Generation Z, otherwise known as the iGeneration and post-Millennials, were born between 1997 and 2012 (Dimock, 2019). While not the only distinguishing factor of this generation, the iPhone launched in 2007, when the oldest Zers were 10. This generation's existence has been defined by technology, mobile devices, WIFI, and digital connectedness. This concept of digital native, truly connected from birth, continues to be a defining characteristic of Generation Z. In addition, diversity is an expectation, and Zers tend to be a little more pragmatic compared to their Millennial counterparts (Lanier, 2017). Finally, in the workplace, employers may have more success dealing with Generation Z through nondigital means because this generation tends to favor in-person communication with leaders (Schawbel, 2014). Generation Z will certainly continue to have a significant impact on 21st century workplaces, especially communication.

Generation Alpha

Generation Alpha currently are characterized by a birth year of 2013 or beyond. As you can imagine, little is known about this generation, and most conclusions are mere conjectures. However, we can project some distinguishing characteristics of this group. First, it is important to note that Alphas are, primarily, the children of Millennials. For those who routinely espouse Millennials as the source of all societal ills, this is bad news. We are already seeing projections of their sheer numbers (Alphas will account for roughly 11% of the global workforce by 2030), and their proclivities, as they are expected to delay life milestones, like marriage and child rearing, similar to previous generations. We may also be able to assume some other distinctions, specifically the influence of technology and constant connection and the formative experience of a global pandemic. While it would not be helpful at this time to determine how Generation Alpha will impact the workforce and workplace, it is worth noting that, like generations before them, they will bring changes, likely ones that are holistic and sweeping. This means workplaces should be continually adept at integrating new generations. The cycle will never end.

Integrating Generations

Pollak (2019) believes that a strong organizational culture is key to combating generational prejudice. She gives great advice when determining how to integrate generations in the workplace. Pollak (2019) says employers should

> Have as open conversation with people as possible with multi-generational employees at all levels about what flexibility means to them. Once you know what people want, you can prioritize what flexible options you can decide to offer. The data can show priority, then you can expand and regroup. (p. 230)

Pollak (2019) touches on a key concept of the future workplace: flexibility. While we can never truly combat or solve those challenges that stare down workplaces in a post-2020 world, we can solve some of those challenges by creating flexible work environments and by talking to our people about their needs and wants. In this vein, we can structure training to address automation and AI, create initiatives to encourage well-being, and deliver an environment where collaboration is not bound by time or geography. A workplace with different generations can be helpful as the organization navigates an ever-evolving set of challenges.

A Culture of Generational Understanding

To their credit, Lyons and LeBlanc (2019) view generational differences from the perspective of identity, not just demographic characteristics. This is helpful because, as they argue, it can reduce stereotypes and even intergenerational conflict (Lyons and LeBlanc, 2019). Ultimately, it is important to remember that every individual is not identified solely by their generational typology and, instead, individuals possess unique desires, especially regarding their careers. A study reiterates three distinct areas where generations differ: work ethic, managing change, and perception of organizational hierarchy (Glass, 2007). These realities may always exist; however, as younger generations become more ingrained in workplace dynamics, these differences may become less pronounced. Until then, organizations would do well to develop a corporate vision that enhances a welcoming understanding of all generations while placing people, no matter their age or generational affiliation, into an environment where they can succeed. Collaborative decision-making and training programs that focus on generational differences from a strengths perspective can also be helpful. Finally, organizations would do well to reconsider their communication efforts and ensure an environment of effective communication.

11.3 Communication "Next"

Effective communication must be a central component of the organization, now maybe more than ever. The influx of different generations into the workplace and the many demands of our communication time and energy necessitate a thorough yet flexible communication structure. Communication style differences exist between generations, and it is traditionally difficult to communicate across generational differences (Pollak, 2019).

The sheer avenues of communication have become multifaceted. Producing a strategy that effectively integrates all channels, both internal and external, should be a central feature of organizations as we continue to move forward toward the future of work. Leaders today should communicate early, communicate often, and communicate with transparency, when appropriate. Specifically, this means inclusive communication and engagement across levels and with employees of varying communication styles should be characteristic of leaders today. In addition, supervisors should actively look for ways to provide feedback, in person and virtually depending on the general tone and tenor of the organization.

The core communication trait needed today is adaptability. Leaders, managers, and employees should recognize that, like leadership, communication is not a one size fits all directive. Instead, people have individual communication preferences. Our current age of work should be approached with self-assessment and analysis. How do you prefer to have others communicate with you? Are you more formal or informal? Do you prefer email, phone, or face-to-face conversations? How do you prefer to receive (and offer) feedback? What level of detail do you desire when you receive messages? Asking yourself these questions and then asking these questions of your employees can help create a strategic communication climate.

As we navigate the future of work, we may also have an opportunity to return to the basics of communication. The channels will change, as they always have, but the core concepts remain the same. Effective communication continues to emphasize simplicity, clarity, and appropriate brevity. In addition, we will continue to see a shift in multimodal communication. Employee preferences for audio, video, and generally more visual communication may continue to increase because of the influx of younger generations but also because our habits and patterns societally are evolving. Organizations, then, would be wise to continue to communicate in ways that reflect broader cultural distinctives without forsaking core tenants.

11.4 Conclusion

There is much we do not know about the future of work, communication next steps, and how generational differences will continue to manifest and influence the organization. However, what we do know is that the workplace will continue to evolve. Organizations will change and adapt. Even in the midst of this evolution, though, employees will continue to search for jobs; companies will be defined by their organizational culture; organizational identification, mentorship, and supportive workplace communication will influence job satisfaction; and dissent and conflict will continue to be present in all organizations.

These organizational and communication variables are key features of work in the past, present, and future. As such, scholars would do well to continue to explore these variables as they relate to remote work, automation and artificial intelligence, well-being, training and development, and inclusivity. The findings presented in this volume provide a crucial starting point, a foundation for generational research at work, but there is more to be done. Our organizations are ripe for additional exploration.

References

Aboobaker, N., Edward, M., & Zakkariya, K. A. (2019). Workplace spirituality, employee wellbeing and intention to stay. *International Journal of Educational Management, 33*, 28–42. doi:10.1108/IJEM-02-2018-004

Autor, D. H. (2015). Why are there still so many jobs? The history and future of workplace automation. *Journal of Economic Perspectives, 29*, 3–30. doi:10.1257/jep.29.3.3

Barnett, R. (2012). Learning for an unknown future. *Higher Education Research and Development, 31*, 65–77.

Bessen, J. (2019). Automation and jobs: When technology boosts employment. *Economic Policy, 34*, 589–626.

Bonk, C., Kim, K., & Zong, T. (2005). Future directions of blended learning in higher education and workplace settings. In C. J. Bonk & C. R. Graham (Eds.), *Handbook of blended learning: Global perspectives, local designs* (pp. 22–25). Pfieffer Publishing.

Carmeli, A., Brueller, D., & Dutton, J. E. (2009). Learning behaviors in the workplace: The role of high-quality interpersonal relationships and psychological safety. *Systems Research and Behavioral Science: The Official Journal of the International Federation for Systems Research, 26*, 81–98. https://doi.org/10.1002/sres.932

Chambel, M. J., & Sobral, F. (2011). Training is an investment with return in temporary workers: A social exchange perspective. *Career Development International, 16*, 161–177.

Davidson, C. (2009). *Future of learning institutions in the digital age.* MacArthur.

Dignan, L. (2011). Cloud computing's real creative destruction may be the IT workforce. ZDNet. Retrieved from: https://www.zdnet.com/article/cloud-computings-real-creative-destruction-may-be-the-it-workforce/

Dimock, M. (2019). Defining generations: Where Millennials end and Generation Z begins. *Pew Research Center, 17*, 1–7.

Dodge, R., Daly, A., Huyton, J., & Sanders, L. (2012). The challenge of defining wellbeing. *International Journal of Wellbeing, 2*, 222–235.

Drucker, P. J. (2000). Knowledge work. *Executive Excellence, 17*, 11–12.

Gallaugher, J. (2014). *Information systems: A Manager's guide to harnessing technology.* Flat World Knowledge

Glass, A. (2007). Understanding generational differences for competitive success. *Industrial and Commercial Trainings, 39,* 90–103.

Hadjileontiadou, S. J., Dias, S. B., Diniz, J. A., & Hadjileontiadis, L. J. (2015). Computer-supported collaborative learning: A holistic perspective. In L. A. Tomei (Ed.), *Fuzzy logic-based modeling in collaborative and blended learning, advances in educational technologies and instructional design* (pp. 51–88). IGI Global

Haenlein, M., & Kaplan, A. (2019). A brief history of artificial intelligence: On the past, present, and future of artificial intelligence. *California Management Review, 6,* 5–14. https://doi.org/10.1177/0008125619864925

Hamilton Skurak, H., Malinen, S., Näswall, K., & Kuntz, J. C. (2018). Employee wellbeing: The role of psychological detachment on the relationship between engagement and work–life conflict. *Economic and Industrial Democracy,* 1–26. https://doi.org/10.1177%2F0143831X17750473

Howard, J. (2019). Artificial intelligence: Implications for the future of work. *American Journal of Industrial Medicine, 62,* 917–926. https://doi.org/10.1002/ajim.23037

Kaplan, A., & Haenlein, M. (2019). Siri, Siri, in my hand: Who's the fairest in the land? On the interpretations, illustrations, and implications of artificial intelligence. *Business Horizons, 62,* 15–25.

Lanier, K. (2017). 5 things HR professionals need to know about Generation Z: Thought leaders share their views on the HR profession and its direction for the future. *Strategic HR Review, 16,* 288–290. https://doi.org/10.1108/SHR-08-2017-0051

Lyons, S. T., & LeBlanc, J. E. (2019). Generational identity in the workplace: Toward understanding and empathy. In R. J. Burke and A. M. Richardsen (Eds.), *Creating psychologically healthy workplaces* (pp. 270–291). Edward Elgar Publishing.

McBride, K. (2020, June 17). Training and development in a post-COVID-19 workplace. *Training Industry.* https://trainingindustry.com/blog/strategy-alignment-and-planning/training-and-development-in-a-post-covid-19-workplace/

Offerman, I. R., & Basford, T. E. (2014). Best practices and the changing role of human resources. In B. M. Ferdman & B. R. Deane (Eds.), *Diversity at work: The practice of inclusion* (pp. 580–592). Jossey-Bass.

Peiró, J. M., Kozusznik, M. W., Rodríguez-Molina, I., & Tordera, N. (2019). The happy-productive worker model and beyond: Patterns of wellbeing and performance at work. *International Journal of Environmental Research and Public Health, 16,* 479–499. https://doi.org/10.3390/ijerph16030479

Peters, M. A. (2017). Technological unemployment: Educating for the fourth industrial revolution. *Educational Philosophy and Theory, 49.* 1–6. doi:10.1080/00131857.2016.1177412

142   *Innovation and Future Challenges*

Pollak, L. (2019). *The remix: How to lead and succeed in the multigenerational workplace.* HarperCollins.

Qin, L., Hsu, J., & Stern, M. (2016). Evaluating the usage of cloud-based collaboration services through teamwork. *Journal of Education for Business, 91,* 227–235. https://doi.org/10.1080/08832323.2016.1170656

Rezai, M., Kolne, K., Bui, S., & Lindsay, S. (2020). Measures of workplace inclusion: A systematic review using the COSMIN methodology. *Journal of Occupational Rehabilitation, 30,* 1–35.

Sako, M. (2020). Artificial intelligence and the future of professional work: Considering the implications of the influence of artificial intelligence given previous industrial revolutions. *Communications of the ACM, 63,* 25–27. https://doi.org/10.1145/3382743

Sabharwal, M. (2014). Is diversity management sufficient? Organizational inclusion to further performance. *Public Personnel Management, 43,* 197–217. http://dx.doi.org/10.1177/0091026014522202

Schawbel, D. (2014, September 2). Gen Y and Gen Z global workplace expectations study. *Workplace Intelligence.* http://millennialbranding.com/2014/geny-genz-global-workplace-expectations-study

Scurtu, L. E. (2015). Knowledge and their shelf life in the business cycle. *Ecoforum 4,* 1–3.

Shore, L. M., Cleveland, J. N., & Sanchez, D. (2018). Inclusive workplaces: A review and model. *Human Resource Management Review, 28*(2), 176–189.

Wang, P. (2019). On Defining Artificial Intelligence. *Journal of Artificial General Intelligence, 10,* 1–37.

Winick, E. (2018, January 25). Every study we could find on what automation will do to jobs, in one chart. *MIT Technology Review.* https://www.technologyreview.com/2018/01/25/146020/every-study-we-could-find-on-what-automation-will-do-to-jobs-in-one-chart/

Index

Note: Page numbers in **bold** indicate tables in the text.

Printed in the United States
by Baker & Taylor Publisher Services